DIANA'S
SECRET LONDON

Published by John Blake Publishing Ltd,
3 Bramber Court, 2 Bramber Road,
London W14 9PB, England

www.johnblakepublishing.co.uk

First published in paperback in 2010

ISBN: 978-1-84454-803-3

British Library Cataloguing-in-Publication Data:
A catalogue record for this book is available from the British Library.

Design by www.envydesign.co.uk

Printed in Great Britain by CPI Bookmarque, Croydon, CR0 4TD

1 3 5 7 9 10 8 6 4 2

Papers used by John Blake Publishing are natural,
recyclable products made from wood grown in sustainable forests.
The manufacturing processes conform to the environmental
regulations of the country of origin.

All venue opening times are correct at time of publication.
Please check with venue for updates.

DIANA'S
SECRET LONDON

Mark Saunders and Glenn Harvey

JOHN BLAKE

With love to Laurie, Alex, Holly, and Victoria

Thanks
For invaluable help and support we would like to thank:
Abdul Daoud, Lucas Constantinou, Michael Cole,
Monica Sniezka, Jasmine Saunders, Richard Cox,
Keith Badman, James Whitaker, June Harvey,
Mervyn Harvey, Margaret Tyler
and Victoria Tabachnikova.

Contents

Introduction

*'By seeing London, I have seen as much of life as
the world can show.'* – Samuel Johnson

IT IS NOT for no reason that when they talk of the three greatest cities on earth London always comes first. Paris, the city of love, and New York, the city that never sleeps, can't offer what London can. London, with 2,000 years of history, heritage and culture seeping from every street, truly is the world's capital city.

The historical superiority of London is enormous: in 1788, when New York became the first capital of the USA, London was already capital of a global empire; in 1789, when an unruly Paris mob were storming the Bastille, singing 'Vive la revolution', London was already the centre of the industrial revolution – perhaps the greatest revolution the world has ever seen.

Whatever happens in this world, London has seen it, done it and probably manufactured the T-shirt. The city has suffered plague, fire, civil unrest, bombardment and terrorist attack, yet, like an ageing pugilist, it refuses to stay down.

London is an exotic madam, an Oxbridge Don, a titled peer and an irascible dandy. It is a sprawling, cosmopolitan mass with no discernible centre. Centuries of urban growth and tourism have transformed it all into a melting pot of culture, hedonism and history; a modern-day Rome in the heart of Babylon, as rewarding as it is challenging. It is a multicultural riot of diversity where more than 300 languages are spoken but one language dominates. It is a confused, overwhelming and vast muddle dominated by scores of world-famous buildings and iconic landmarks; one sweeping glance will take in Tower Bridge, The Houses of Parliament, Tower of London, Westminster Abbey, Buckingham Palace and Trafalgar Square. Thirty-nine per cent of the total area of London is green, and there are more parks and green spaces than any other city of its size.

London's merits go on and on like the city itself: the most powerful financial centre in the world, the largest nightlife district in the world, the largest airport in the world, the most prestigious and famous shopping in the world, arguably the sports capital of the world (London contains more sports stadiums than any other city on earth and is home to the football Mecca of Wembley Stadium), the oldest and longest subway network in the world and, as if all of that's not enough, it is home to the oldest and most famous monarchy in the world.

In short, London is today how Joseph Conrad described it more than a hundred years ago: 'the biggest, and the greatest, town on earth'.

Princess Diana's London, by contrast, was relatively small; the area Diana made her own, known colloquially as the 'Tiara Triangle', stretched from Kensington in the west as far south as Fulham, north-east to Mayfair and back west to Kensington.

London was Diana's city. She knew it like the back of her hand. Indeed, so extensive was her knowledge of its traffic-choked streets that, *in another world*, she could easily have been a London cabbie.

Diana arrived in London in 1979 as a naive, somewhat gawky, 18-year-old. For two years she led *la dolce vita* from a flat in West Fulham, becoming the most famous of all the Sloane Rangers, before marrying the Prince of Wales and discovering London was not just her oyster, it was the pearl inside as well.

After her separation, Diana chose to stay in London. Despite being the most famous person in the world, she found an anonymity among the throbbing, vibrant mass of people. She loved the seasonal street vendors, hawking everything from strawberries to roasted chestnuts; the huge cinemas with their dazzling daytime neon heralding the arrival of the latest blockbuster; and the never-ending chain of globally recognised brands that scream out from every shop window.

Among this teeming metropolis, and away from the prying eyes of the press, Diana enjoyed two love affairs and a freedom very few realised, and certainly one that very few celebrities have enjoyed.

This book tells the story of Diana's London, from the majestic glory of the most famous royal homes to those secret places where she laughed, loved and played. Diana's London life was unique and probably unlike any life lived before. One moment she would be on the balcony at Buckingham Palace, alongside the Queen and Prince Charles, the next she would be driving alone through the rear gates of Kensington Palace, heading for a girly lunch and an afternoon's shopping.

This book has been structured as a walking tour to allow both the Diana fan and the simple tourist to enjoy the very best

London has to offer. London is a journey of discovery and we hope this book will point you in the right direction.

But always remember, discovering London is like opening a Pandora's box of the most famous and historic sights in the world; no matter what you see or where you are, there's always something better round the corner. It's not unlike looking up a favourite song on YouTube then delving into those addictive related videos on the sidebar. Three hours after your original quest to find an old Bay City Rollers hit, you're engrossed in the Battle of Stalingrad.

London works the same way. What starts off as a couple of hours at the National Gallery will end many hours later sipping wine on the South Bank, somehow managing to have taken in Trafalgar Square, Big Ben, Parliament, 10 Downing Street, Covent Garden, St Paul's Cathedral, Tower Bridge *and* the Tower of London on the way.

All this *and* Diana too.

WALK I

THIS WALK INCLUDES:

A coffee break to start / A visit to Kensington
Palace, London home of Princess Diana / Diana's
high-street shopping / A walk through Kensington
Gardens / A section of the Diana, Princess of Wales
Memorial Walk / The Diana, Princess of Wales
Memorial Fountain

Length – *3.5 miles or 5.4 km*
Time – *4 hours, excluding the visit to*
Kensington Palace
Underground – *Queensway or Notting Hill Gate*
Bus routes – *70, 94, 148 and 390 go to*
Bayswater Road. Request Kensington
Palace Gardens

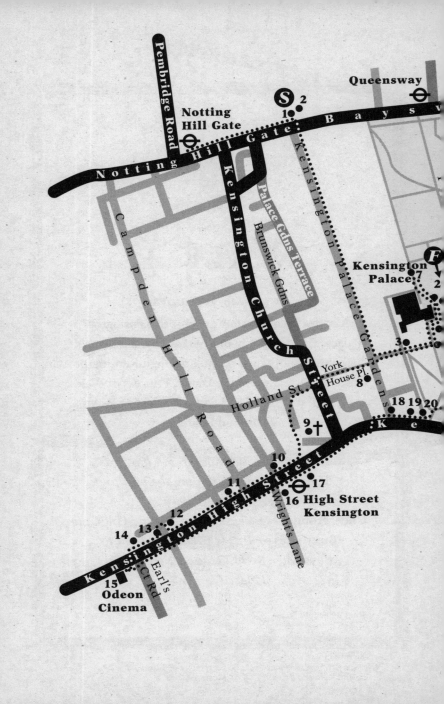

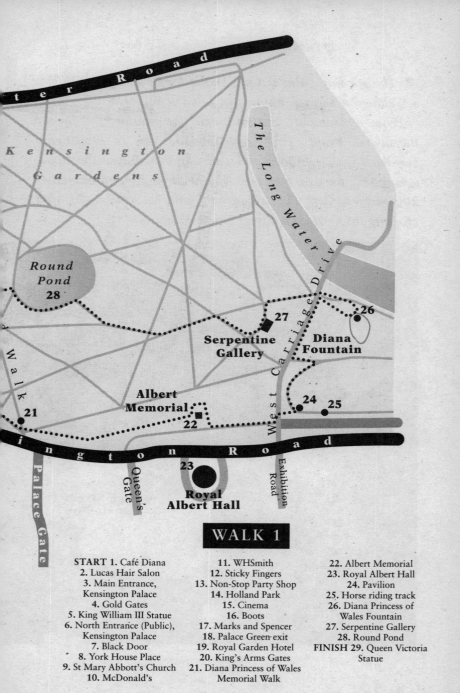

WALK 1

☞ *The starting point is Café Diana (open at 8.30am daily), 5 Wellington Terrace, Bayswater, London W2 4LW.*

From Queensway Station, exit the station on to the Bayswater Road. The park opposite you is Kensington Gardens. Turn right/west and walk along the Bayswater Road, keeping the park on your left. After walking for approximately 200 metres, Café Diana can be found on your right after crossing the Ossington Street junction.

From Notting Hill Gate, exit the station and turn left. Walk along Notting Hill Gate eastwards. After 400 metres and after the junction with Clanricarde Gardens, Café Diana is on your left.

Starting point – Café Diana

Café Diana is a small, unpretentious establishment on the Bayswater Road and, if the public's love for Princess Diana has a soul, it is to be found here. The café is owned by Abdul Basit

Daoud, a jovial Iraqi who is among the few people in the world that could genuinely call Diana a friend.

The café was opened on 6 January 1989, its name inspired by the proximity of Kensington's most famous resident, who lived literally just across the street.

Abdul had toyed with a number of names, including the Notting Hill Café and Abduls, before settling on the simple, yet evocative, Café Diana.

In the beginning business was brisk. Tourists would inevitably stop at the small café before treading the well-worn path around Kensington Palace. In Abdul they found a friend, his amiable, jolly manner, his constant smiles, the perfect host for breakfast prior to a good day's sightseeing.

The staff at Café Diana were always ready to welcome a special guest in for coffee. Reproduced with kind permission © Abdul Basit Daoud.

Abdul was no novice to running a successful café or serving famous people. Back home in Baghdad, he had run one of the most famous bars in the city with his father. 'I remember this one chap who used to come in with his bodyguard,' Abdul says. 'He was a bad man … very evil eyes. His name was Saddam Hussein.' Nearly 20 years later, that 'bad man' was executed by the people of Iraq for crimes against humanity, leaving Abdul with the dubious honour of being the only man on earth to have served a kebab to the personification of good and the personification of evil.

Abdul had no idea what Diana would think of his little enterprise. In the beginning he was concerned she may feel her name was being somewhat reduced in stature, hanging over the doorway of a small café but his worries were completely unfounded. Each morning Diana would leave the rear exit of Kensington Palace, glance across at the small café that bore her name and say the same thing to her personal protection officer Ken Wharfe. 'One day, Ken, I'm going to go in there.'

When Diana did eventually come into the café, Abdul was so shocked he hid behind the coffee machine.

'I couldn't believe it,' he says with a beaming smile, the memory as fresh today as it was 20 years ago when he first saw her. 'I was making coffee when I glanced up at the door and there she was. I didn't know what to do … so, naturally, I hid.'

Diana loitered in the doorway with Ken Wharfe. Abdul's Hungarian assistant showed none of the reluctance to meet the Princess that her boss was showing and greeted Diana with a huge smile. 'Darlink,' she said. 'How good to see you.'

The waitress took their order of an espresso for Ken Wharfe and a cappuccino for Diana, and showed them to a table.

KENSINGTON PALACE

1 July 1997

Dear Abdul,

I wanted to write personally, to thank you so very much for the beautiful flowers you sent for my birthday. They truly are quite magnificent and I am deeply touched that you have thought of me in this special way.

With my very kindest regards and warmest good wishes,

Diana

Café Diana

Above: One of many personal letters sent from Diana to Café Diana.

Left: Abdul Basit Daoud sits before his Diana photo gallery inside Café Diana. Reproduced with kind permission, © Abdul Basit Daoud.

Eventually Abdul was coaxed out of his hiding place behind the coffee machine. 'I went across to Diana's table and perched myself at the end. I had no idea what I was supposed to do or say … how do you greet royalty when they've just sat down in your café?' he says with a grin.

Within moments, however, Diana had swept away all of Abdul's fears, greeting him with a smile that radiated friendship, putting him so at ease that he felt she was a familiar friend rather than a

Princess. 'She was incredible,' he says. 'Her laugh was so infectious.'

Abdul beamed with pride as Diana told him she approved of the café being named after her.

After that, Diana became a regular. Usually, when she took William and Harry to the barber's shop next door, she would pop in to see him and share a cappuccino. 'She always sat at the same table,' says Abdul, pointing it out. 'The tourists that come here now have no idea they are sitting in the same spot Diana used to enjoy her coffee ... oh, you should see their faces when I tell them.'

Diana never expected special treatment at the café. 'She insisted on being treated like any other customer,' Abdul says. 'If we were crowded (which was very often) she would wait her turn for a table like anyone else.'

On one occasion, Diana was sitting in her usual spot when a woman on the table behind asked her to pass the ketchup. 'Diana thought it was hilarious,' says Abdul. 'Oh, now I'm the waitress,' she said, laughing as she handed over the bottle.

Another time, Diana met one of Abdul's regular customers, a clairvoyant, who offered to read her palm. Diana turned the offer down, saying at that time that the future was so unpredictable she would be terrified to know anything about it.

Before long, Diana began to bring William and Harry into the café, making a foursome along with Ken Wharfe at her usual table. 'William and Harry were so polite,' says Abdul. 'They were like perfect little gentlemen. For them it was a big treat being allowed into the café; they were always so excited.'

On one memorable occasion, Harry came in on his own with his mum. Abdul treated him to some sweets and Harry shouted, 'William will be so jealous ... I can't wait to tell him.'

Abdul immediately made up a small packet of sweets for William, which included two Kit-Kats. The following morning he was surprised to see the car that drove William and Harry on the school run stop in the middle of the road outside his shop. 'I looked out and saw William winding down the rear window,' he says. 'I thought he was going to wave, like they did every morning, but instead he beckoned me over.' Abdul went over to the car and William thanked him profusely for the sweets. 'It was a lovely gesture,' says Abdul. 'He didn't have to do it then. He could have waited until he came in next time … but that's the sort of person he is, just like his mother.'

Diana would often send notes and flowers to Abdul; if she was due to be away for any length of time she would apologise for not seeing him in advance and promise to pop in as soon as she got back.

'One time, I sent her a letter,' Abdul says. 'I had read in the papers about her divorce and various other emotional problems she was having. So I wrote a simple letter reminding her she was a good person and that one day her troubles would be behind her.'

Abdul did not expect a reply. He wrote the letter as a genuine act of compassion. The following day he received a phone call from Diana. 'She wanted to thank me personally for my message,' he says. 'Then she told me she would be coming into the café tomorrow. I told her I had a small infection and was having problems with my voice. She replied, "Don't tell anyone I'm coming or you'll lose your voice for ever."'

Diana came to the café as arranged. It was to be her longest visit. 'We sat and chatted for ages,' Abdul recalls. 'I got the feeling Diana didn't want to leave. At that time the papers were full of news about her divorce. She was so sad. She told me, "I never wanted a divorce, Abdul ... I come from a divorced family myself and it's awful for the children."'

Diana revealed to Abdul that she was cutting back all her charity work. 'I just can't cope with so much,' she said sadly. 'I have to work with over a hundred different charities and it's just too much.'

By this time Abdul had begun decorating the walls of Café Diana with photos of its unofficial patron. Diana would look the photos over – some she approved of and others made her wince. 'It always seemed so strange talking to a woman whose photos covered all the walls,' Abdul says. 'I was aware many of the photos had been taken by the dreaded paparazzi but Diana didn't seem to care. "Oh, them," she would say dryly as she waved her hand in a dismissive manner.'

Diana always insisted on paying for her coffee. 'She wouldn't have it any other way,' says Abdul. 'There was no point trying. On a couple of occasions I insisted it was "my treat" but most of the time she would rummage into her handbag and produce a note.'

Though the notes were handed over and the change given, Diana's cash rarely made it to the bank. 'The staff would always keep them as a souvenir,' he says, laughing. 'Proudly keeping them at home and showing them off ... It's not many people that can say they've been given a £5 note by royalty.'

Abdul last saw Diana two weeks before she died. 'She had popped in to say it looked like she'd be away for a while, and to wish us all a good summer,' says Abdul. 'I remember she was wearing a grey suit and looked particularly beautiful. As she left she glanced at the photos on the wall and said, "Isn't this enough photos?" And those were the last words she ever said to me.'

Like all of Diana's close friends, Abdul has a story about her death but it is personal and private, and does not need repeating here. But what can be said is that, in a remarkable gesture by a remarkable man, Abdul refused to open Café Diana for two days after her death. At a time when he could have made thousands out of the vast crowds that had flocked to Kensington, Abdul chose instead to hand out free water to the various police officers and officials involved in organising the crowds, and keep the café shut as a mark of respect.

'She supported me in life,' Abdul says. 'And I continue to support her in death.' Abduls words are moving and honest. His café is now a tribute to Diana that she would have been proud of. When people first come in they look at the photos on the wall and smile. 'And that's what I want,' says Abdul. 'Diana always made people smile … and in my little café she still does.'

☞ *Step out from Café Diana and turn left, walk 10 metres. After passing two shop fronts you will find Lucas Hair Salon.*

Lucas Hair Salon – William's and Harry's barber

Next door but one to Café Diana is Lucas Hair Salon, where Diana would frequently take William and Harry to have their hair cut. It is owned by Lucas Constantinou, a suave, well-mannered, silver-haired Greek who would not look out of place on a yacht in the Mediterranean. Indeed, the whole shop is so Mediterranean in its ambience you can almost hear the haunting beauty of the theme from *Zorba The Greek* as you walk through the door. The barber shop was popular with many of the staff at Kensington Palace because of its close proximity, literally a stone's throw from many of the servants' quarters or 'a 5 iron' from Diana's front door.

Diana first brought William and Harry here in 1993, prior to a trip to the West End to see the movie *Jurassic Park*. She had been told of the place by her butler Paul Burrell.

Lucas is stunningly good looking in a Greek George Clooney sort of way. He talks proudly yet quietly of his friendship with Diana as he continues to cut the hair of favoured clients. In the ten years since Diana's death, Lucas has watched his clientele change, get older, move on. He still gets new customers asking if this was the place Prince William used to get his hair cut, the person doing the asking completely unaware that the hands cutting her hair are the same that cut William's and Harry's.

'Diana was a beautiful person,' reminisces Lucas. 'And I don't just mean physically. She was beautiful inside. When she spoke to you, she had a knack of making you feel like a lifelong friend. You would never have dreamed she was a princess.'

As William or Harry sat in the barbers chair furthest away from the main door (a deliberate ploy by Lucas to keep them away from the prying eyes of the paparazzi), Diana would pull up a chair and sit alongside them.

'She was just like any other customer,' said Lucas. 'When the boys first sat down I would ask what she wanted me to do and she would always say, "Keep it simple." It was always Harry who would ask for a "skinhead" or to have his hair dyed green. Diana would laugh and say, "Oh, the press would just *love* that."' As Lucas cut the boys' hair, they would talk of movies or football. 'They were just like any other young boys,' he said. 'Especially William. He was so friendly and so naturally at ease, it was sometimes hard to believe I was cutting the hair of the future King of England.

'Sometimes the boys would come to the shop without their mother. Usually one of the royal detectives, either Steve Brown or Ken Wharfe, would pop across the road and put their head round the door and ask, "Everything OK?" That was the signal that William or Harry would be coming over.'

Despite her royal status, neither Diana nor the boys received any form of special treatment from Lucas or his staff. 'If we were busy they would wait their turn like everyone else,' he says. 'Diana never wanted, nor expected, any special favours.'

As Lucas talks of Diana, his face takes on the same expression as that of Abdul next door. Wistfully, he looks across the road towards Kensington Palace, a faraway look in his eye, a thousand memories crossing his mind. 'I miss her,' he says. 'I miss her so much. What I loved most about Diana was her spontaneity, her love of life and her love of laughing. Her laughter was infectious; once she started she could never stop and within moments the whole shop would be creasing up.'

There is nothing made up about Lucas's friendship with Diana. He has photos of her with the boys in his shop. When asked for permission to publish them, he says no. 'They are personal memories of a beautiful person,' he says. 'And I would rather keep them to myself.'

When asked what he feels about the break-up of Diana's marriage, Lucas responds as only genuine friends of Diana always do. 'Marriages sometimes don't work,' he says. 'Charles and Diana were no different to 50 per cent of the people who get married in this country today. In any divorce you will always get two sides to the same story and somewhere in the middle will be the truth. The Diana I knew was a happily married woman who lived for her children ... and that is how I will always remember her.'

☞ *With Lucas Hair Salon behind you, look across the road towards a road entrance with white arches and pillars. Cross the road and enter the left-hand pedestrian archway.*

Kensington Palace Gardens – Embassy Row

Crossing the road from Lucas Hair Salon, you will see the large black wrought-iron gates and heavily guarded sentry box that heralds the start of Kensington Palace Gardens, a tree-lined avenue, half a mile long, that runs parallel with Kensington Palace and is home to more than fifty embassies from all over the world. It is one of the most expensive residential streets on earth and has long been known as 'Billionaires' Row' due to the wealth of its private residents. It is immediately to the west of Kensington Gardens and connects Notting Hill Gate to Kensington High Street. Kensington Palace Gardens is, without doubt, one of the most intriguing places to live in the whole of London. It is a fascinating street, for inside the vast mansions that fly their countries' flags is a James Bond world of skulduggery, spying, beautiful woman and titled ambassadors; a world where political assassinations are planned, counter-surveillance is carried out and a whole host of characters plucked straight from the pages of a John Le Carre novel go about their daily business. The rooms of every building are routinely swept for bugs and the shifty-looking characters you see parked in Range Rovers with blacked-out windows work for MI5, CIA, Mossad and various other 'friendly' secret services.

Kensington Palace Gardens began life in the 1840s on part of the grounds of Kensington Palace and to this day the freehold belongs to the Crown Estate. Aficionados of architecture will note that the exquisitely beautiful houses at the northern end (Bayswater) are mostly Italianate, while those at the southern end are generally in the more boring Queen Anne style. Although the majority of the houses are occupied by embassies, many have been renovated by the Crown Estate and sold to private buyers on long leases. One of these, number 18–19, is well worth a look. It was bought in 2004 by the Indian steel tycoon Lakshmi Mittal, who in 2008 was listed by *Forbes* magazine as the fourth richest man in the world. Formerly, Bernie Ecclestone, the Formula One racing boss, owned the house. On 8 October 2001, Bernie purchased the house from Iranian scholar and philanthropist David Khalili for £50 million. However, it was widely reported that Bernie's wife, Slavica, never liked the 55,000sq-ft, 18-bedroomed mansion, and they never moved in. Khalili spent three years and more than £20 million turning the two houses into one, building a swimming pool and indulging his taste for marble floors and pillars (using marble excavated from the same quarry as that used for the Taj Mahal). Paul Reuter, the founder of the Reuters news agency, was also a former resident.

But, without doubt, the most intriguing address in the street is number 8, for this was the location of the notorious 'London Cage', the British Government's torture centre used during World War II and the Cold War. The Cage was run by MI9, a division of British Military Intelligence, part of the War Office. In World War II, it was responsible for obtaining information from enemy prisoners of war.

Princess Diana would often use the Bayswater exit if she was visiting friends in Holland Park or heading towards Park Lane and Belgravia. Sometimes it would be a convenient way to avoid the rush-hour traffic in Kensington High Street. Although Diana always insisted she wanted no special treatment just because she was a member of the Royal Family, she did make use of the Metropolitan Police radios tucked into the lapels of the officers of the Royal Protection Squad. As she drove out of the courtyard of Kensington Palace, Diana would stop at the first sentry box and ask the officer on duty to check on the traffic situation, and then decide which exit to use.

☞ *Walk down Kensington Palace Gardens for 500 metres and, across a large area of grass, you can see Kensington Palace.*

Princess Diana's home, Kensington Palace (KP) as seen from Kensington Palace Gardens.

Kensington Palace

In 1981, when Charles and Diana first moved into Kensington Palace, *The House of Windsor* was the longest-running and most-watched 'soap opera' in the world. But critics were suggesting it had become boring. A successful soap needs a constant reinvention of character and storyline in order to maintain interest; nothing exciting had happened in *The House of Windsor* since the abdication of King Edward VIII nearly half a century before. True, there had been one or two moments when audience figures topped a billion; the Queen's coronation in 1952, for example, or the investiture of a young Prince Charles as the Prince of Wales and, of course, some excellent scandal involving a young Princess Margaret and a dashing RAF Pilot Group Captain Townsend but, on the whole, *The House of Windsor* plodded along like a royal version of *The Archers*, cropping up only in conversation when someone said, 'Oh, is that *still* going?'

The show had originally been called *The Royals*, and was an Anglo-French production which was first aired in 1066. Its first smashing episode opened with a battle, a real battle, a magnificent battle of such significance it changed the face of world history. Oh, there was no expense spared in those days. The battle was fought at Hastings between the show's first foreign heartthrob, William the Conqueror, and a gallant English King named Harold. In boxing terms, this would have been the Ali/Frazier of its day, and it was a phenomenal success. True, the plot *was* complicated and one of the show's leading men, Harold, died in the first episode, but *The Royals*, an every-day saga of life in the Royal Family, was just what a jaded population emerging from the dark ages needed.

The Royals is to British history what the twelve-bar is to rock-'n'roll, and the show remains the template for every soap ever made. The whole point of a good soap is to allow the audience to belong to a world they'll never know and, certainly, *The Royals* lived in a world totally detached from reality. But in an age when people finally had the chance to settle down at the end of the day rather than fight off heathen Viking raiders, *The Royals* proved an immediate hit, with an intrepid cast of kings and queens, heroes and villains, and cameos from some of the most famous people in history.

In the early days, each episode would unfold from the lips of storytellers who would travel the country with tales of love, war and infidelity among the ruling classes. Though the stories were certainly risqué (even in the 11th century the public wanted a fair share of bonking among the action), the authors had to be careful what they said, for those who insulted the monarch usually met with a grisly death that involved having parts of the anatomy sliced off with hot irons.

Like all good soaps, the cast changed frequently but the plots remained the same. In the beginning 'boy gets throne, boy loses throne, boy gets throne back again' was a typical storyline as an outrageous and unbelievable number of cutthroats, rogues and murderers fought for supremacy of Britain.

William the Conqueror was the first real *star* of the show but he was by no means the most famous. Indeed, fame for the leading players of *The Royals* got bigger and better every time communication improved. By the reign of Elizabeth I, America had entered the storyline; the English Navy ruled the waves (and thus England ruled the world) and *The Royals* was bigger than The Beatles, despite the best efforts of rival soaps from Spain, France and the Roman Catholic Church.

The success of *The Royals* was obvious; there has never been a show with such a diversity of characters taking over the leading role and each one brought their own unique personality to the star part. They were loved, loathed, hated, heroic, evil and, in more than one case, completely bonkers. *The Royals* had so much *action*; there were battles, wars, fights, squabbles, infidelity, perversion, homicide, fratricide, regicide, genocide, suicide, in some cases all in one episode.

In 1917, *The Royals* changed its named to *The House of Windsor* in a blatant attempt to distract attention away from its

Germanic relations (Britain was at war with Germany at the time). Much confusion was caused among many of the younger cast, who suddenly found their names had changed. The Battenbergs became the Mountbattens and the Tecks, who had a very silly name anyway, became the Cambridges. A by-product of this name change (and the war) was that *The Royals* now had to become terribly British; hitherto, it had pretty much been a European show, with a DNA that spanned two continents. But as the two countries had just lost nearly two million men apiece fighting a war against each other, there were to be no more marriages between English and German dynasties. Marriage with other European monarchs was not exactly outlawed, just very difficult to arrange, as most of the European monarchies were now broke, fragmented or, in the case of the Russians, dead.

Elizabeth II became the star of *The House of Windsor* in 1952 and with her dashing Greek leading man, the Duke of Edinburgh (a genuine war hero), watched the show go from black and white to colour. But, although *The House of Windsor* (like James Bond) remained something uniquely British that the Americans could never better, it had begun to slip down the ratings.

By 1981 it *was* still going but only just, and facing fierce competition from the Palace of Westminster, where a troublesome usurper called Margaret Thatcher had entrenched her armies.

Ironically, it was Thatcher that gave *The House of Windsor* the wake-up call it needed. The show had become complacent, the characters stale. The strange non-emergence of a World War III meant that nearly two generations had grown up virtually intact. War, which was always a good ratings winner for *The Royals*, no longer had monarchs trading 'kingdoms for horses' in the middle of the battlefield; these days it tended to include complete nuclear annihilation, which played hell with the television schedules. Unimaginably, a bizarre role-reversal had taken place between Parliament and the monarchy. Thatcher was prepared to take *her* country to war again to make *her* country great again; the monarch wanted peace to preserve the ever-dwindling common-wealth *and* Planet Earth. Both sides were to come up with extraordinarily brilliant schemes to further their cause.

In 1982, Thatcher got her war, basked in the glory of liberating some faraway islands predominantly populated by penguins, it appeared, for a short while, that the tanks really would roll up The Mall and surround Buckingham Palace. Being Prime Minister was not enough for Margaret Thatcher; she wanted the world, baby, and everything in it.

But though *The House of Windsor* was down, it was far from out.

The year before Thatcher's war, *The House of Windsor* did what soaps always do for a quick ratings fix – they had a wedding. But this wasn't any old wedding. Oh no … this was the biggest, grandest, most watched and celebrated wedding in history. More than a billion people saw the marriage of Charles, Prince of Wales, to Lady Diana Spencer, and the birth of the biggest star *The Royals* or *The House of Windsor* has ever produced – Princess Diana. Thatcher's metaphorical tanks beat a hasty retreat back up The Mall as *The House of Windsor* once again reigned supreme as the world's favourite soap.

They then did something that, though quite common by the end of the decade, was virtually unheard of in 1981. For the first time in its history, *The Royals/The House of Windsor* produced a highly rated spin-off that was to eventually become bigger than the mother-show itself.

The show was called *Kensington Palace*, which, in the great tradition of all soaps, was immediately shortened to *KP* (see page 1 plate section).

☞ *Continue for a further 200 metres and, when the railings end, turn left into Palace Green. Walk along Palace Green and you will pass the main entrance security gates on your left. Cross over Palace Avenue and enter Kensington Gardens through Studio Gate ahead of you, all the time keeping the Palace on your left.*

Kensington Gardens

Although definitely the smallest of the Royal Parks, Kensington Gardens, like the Palace that took its name, has a special place in the heart of the Royal Family and it is, of course, the park most associated with Princess Diana. Kensington Gardens is only 275 acres and lies in the City of Westminster, adjacent to Hyde Park and between Bayswater and Kensington Road; KP is on the western edge. Most of the land which now forms Kensington Gardens was originally part of Hyde Park. Henry VIII acquired farmland from Westminster Abbey and enclosed it for hunting in 1536. The history of Kensington Gardens, however, really begins in 1689 when William III bought Nottingham House from the Earl of Nottingham together with adjacent land. The house was enlarged and remodelled by Sir Christopher Wren and became Kensington House. William and his wife, Mary II, entrusted the development of the Palace Gardens to George London and Henry Wise.

Under Queen Anne, the gardens were remodelled and extended by Wise to take in an area of gravel pits between the Palace and Bayswater Road, and a deer paddock in Hyde Park. The Orangery was built in a baroque style to a design by Nicholas Hawksmoor and Sir John Vanbrugh. The next and perhaps most influential phase of the development of Kensington Gardens occurred in the late 1720s and early 1730s. It owed much to the interest of George II's wife, Queen Caroline, and the firm direction of Charles Bridgman. The formation of the Round Pond and the Long Water date from this period. Further acres were taken from Hyde Park and included in Kensington Gardens. For a century, no more work took place and Bridgman's planting structure was allowed to deteriorate. Public access was increasingly allowed from the early 19th century and, in the 1840s, the wall was replaced with iron railings like those around Hyde Park.

The Victorian period was notable for the creation of the Italian fountains in 1860 and the building of the Albert Memorial between 1864 and 1872. This splendid Gothic structure designed by George Gilbert Scott was damaged during World War II and its iron roof structure has been badly corroded; it is currently undergoing a major refurbishment by the Department of the Environment.

Kensington Gardens is a much quieter place today than Hyde Park. Much used by local residents, it has strong associations with children. The statue of Peter Pan designed by Sir George Frampton to commemorate JM Barrie's famous character and the Elfin Oak in the playground area, with figures remodelled by the legendary English comedian Spike Milligan, still attract many visitors. Model yachts are sailed on the Round Pond and on the eastern side of the gardens the old tearooms have been

Floral tributes to Princess Diana 1997. Rex Features

successfully converted into the Serpentine Gallery. The notable avenue of Elm Trees flanking the Broad Walk, ravaged by disease, was replanted with limes and Norway maples in 1953. The gardens also suffered heavy losses, like most of the Royal Parks, in the severe storm of October 1987.

☞ *Enter Kensington Palace by the Gold Kensington Palace Gates.*

Gold Gates

Of all the images captured in the immediate aftermath of Princess Diana's death, surely the most powerful is the incredible display of flowers that were laid outside the Gold Gates at Kensington Palace. The first flowers were laid in the early hours of Sunday morning, as the terrible news from Paris was confirmed. In an atmosphere of stunned quiet, people made their way to the Palace. They laid their wreaths and stood silently. Nobody spoke – it was too early for words – instead they stood in tribute to Diana, a woman many of them had never met and yet still loved. People couldn't remember a time when Diana hadn't been in their lives. They had celebrated her wedding, rejoiced at the birth of her children, laughed at her almost irreverent approach to royal duties, grown concerned at her weight loss and offered support when her marriage to Prince Charles irretrievably broke down.

Now they wept. Openly and truthfully. They wept for a woman who had come to be symbolic of their own lives. A woman who, despite having wealth and privilege beyond most people's wildest dreams, had only ever wanted one thing ... love.

In death, Diana discovered love; a huge tidal wave of love given to her by a never-ending river of people who descended on KP that fateful Sunday morning and throughout the week that followed. People flocked in their thousands to lay flowers, cards, messages and even toys and clothing. One woman spoke for everyone when she said, 'I came here for Diana … she was my idol.'

The grief was accompanied by silence … and the silence was eerie. The only sounds were the gentle sobs of people mourning. Never before had such a scene been witnessed in London, or anywhere in the world. People knelt in front of the gates, rosaries in hand, praying for Diana. Others spoke in hushed whispers and nobody could believe that Diana was dead.

It took a pensioner to sum up the feeling that had swept across the country. She laid her flowers near the gates, stood up and looked at the crowds behind her. Eyes glazed, handkerchief in hand, she turned to a small boy standing next to her. 'During the war, every day was like this,' she said.

☞ *Pass the King William III statue. Follow the path around the building, past the Sunken Garden on your right and towards the main entrance located at the north side of the building.*

Diana heads indoors.

Kensington Palace visitor entrance on the north side. On the right is the black doorway (see page 48).

Kensington Palace

There are few royal homes with a history as colourful and as controversial as Kensington Palace. And there are few royal homes so deeply *loved* as Kensington Palace. It seems to have some sort of mesmerising hold over anyone fortunate enough to have lived there. Queen Victoria was born and brought up in the Palace and her love of her childhood home saved it from demolition when it fell into a state of disrepair during the second half of the 19th century. King George V pleaded to be allowed to pull down Buckingham Palace (which he loathed) and, with the money saved, rebuild Kensington Palace as the primary town residence of the sovereign. Princess Diana herself refused to give up her apartment at KP during the protracted divorce negotiations, despite the Queen's offer of any 'reasonably' priced house in London. KP is the most unlikely looking palace in the world. It has none of the majesty of Buckingham Palace or the history of St James's Palace. It doesn't even look like a palace, far closer in resemblance to a Prussian fencing school than a royal home and yet, from 1689, when William III first purchased the Jacobean house, until 1760, when George II did an 'Elvis' and dropped dead on the toilet, Kensington Palace was the much-favoured residence of successive sovereigns. Maybe it's the lack of stuffy, royal protocol so often associated with Buckingham Palace, but KP was the place where everyone let their hair, and their morals, down; consequently, its history is a wonderful kaleidoscope of tantrums, tears, infidelity, drama and death.

Originally called Nottingham House, KP became a royal residence when William III bought it from his Secretary of State, the Earl of Nottingham, in June 1689. The King suffered from chronic asthma, a condition not helped by the rambling Palace of Whitehall on the banks of the River Thames (the official residence of the Tudor and Stuart monarchs), and was determined to move his court further west. When his eye fell on the beautiful Nottingham House, he made the owner an offer he couldn't refuse. The Earl of Nottingham was reluctant to sell as he genuinely loved the place but, unfortunately for him, it was bad form to refuse such a request from the King.

William III was an odd character who sailed remarkably close to the wind – and we're not suggesting he had any nautical leanings. He stood just over five feet tall in his stockinged feet (his oddness included a penchant for women's underwear) and he was hunchbacked, confirming a splendidly royal bloodline. From childhood he had suffered terribly with asthma. When William was 26, he decided to marry his cousin, Mary – as if incest wasn't bad enough, the poor girl was only 15 at the time. In complete despair, Mary wept for days when they informed her she was to marry her asthmatic, hunchbacked, transvestite, paedophile cousin, and she continued to weep during the marriage service itself, which took place in St James's Palace in 1677, on the 27th birthday of her husband/cousin.

Fearing the joy of the ceremony was being somewhat ruined by a weeping bride-to-be, her uncle, King Charles II, tried desperately to cheer Mary up. When the time came for William to say the words 'With all my worldly goods I thee endow', several coins were spread out, ceremonially, on the open bible. Charles whispered to the sobbing Mary, 'Grab them and put them in your pocket while you've still got the chance.' A remark that made the poor girl sob with grief.

Strictly speaking, it was Mary who was next in line to the throne but William, throwing a majestic royal tantrum, openly refused to be subjugated to the role of a mere consort. Poor Mary didn't have any say in the matter, save to agree completely with her husband. Thus, the curious situation arose by which the monarchy was shared between them. In practice, of course, it was William who made all the decisions, though Mary remained in control of the channel changer.

And that was pretty much how the marriage continued. Mary was never allowed any form of opinion unless it was in complete agreement with her husband and, throughout her reign, she remained under his shadow.

And yet, despite her blatant subjugation, Mary's marriage *was* a success. William's terrible asthma caused him to snore intolerably at night so it was decided the royal bed would not be shared. At the Palace of Whitehall, Mary had her own set of chambers to sleep in. This meant the royal couple saw very little of each other once the working day had ended and this probably contributed greatly to the success of their union.

Happily married by living apart, William and Mary had a gay old time. They both patronised the arts, including the by now fashionable art of gardening, and enjoyed the opera. They would often be seen at first nights together and frequently dining at the most fashionable restaurants.

The practice of keeping separate bedrooms continued when the couple finally moved into Kensington Palace. It was a happy occasion. Both shared that sense of excitement, unique to married couples, at having finally achieved a place of their own.

Although Mary and William loved their new home, like most rich people they couldn't resist flaunting their wealth and putting their own stamp on it. Royalty didn't do anything by half in those days, so Christopher Wren was immediately commissioned to extend and improve the house and, keeping with the mantra that only the best will do, Nicholas Hawksmoor was appointed his clerk of works. Annoyingly, this meant that no sooner had Mary and William moved in than they had to move out again, being forced to find alternative accommodation while the work was completed. The two famous architects set to work with gusto following the promise of huge rewards should they finish ahead of schedule, since Mary was impatient to leave her temporary accommodation at nearby Holland House. Despite the ill-omened collapse of a newly built part of the house in November of that year, the court moved back in shortly before Christmas 1689.

Sadly, Mary did not live long to enjoy either her new house or her reign. She died, aged 32 and childless, from smallpox.

Wren's improvements to the old house can be summed up with typical British understatement: 'gigantic!' In fact, it might have been easier to knock the place down and start again. Wren effectively redesigned the entire building. It was hardly your routine household extension.

Wren's work at KP was finally completed in August 1690. In those days it was still known as Kensington House, having been constructed more as a private country house than a royal residence. It was not until later when royal occupants instituted a series of grand and expensive changes that it eventually became known as Kensington Palace.

Queen Anne succeeded William III in 1702 and became the next royal resident at Kensington Palace. If William can be described as odd (and that's being charitable), Anne can only be described as pathetically tragic and terribly unfortunate. She suffered awfully from gout, and she eventually became so fat and heavy that she could hardly move, and had to be pushed, carried and wheeled about, even to the extent of having to be lowered through trap doors. She had an unbelievable 17 miscarriages and stillbirths. When eventually she did give birth successfully, her only child, the sad little Duke of Gloucester, barely made it through childhood and died when he was 11.

Anne was reportedly the most boring woman on earth, married to King George of Denmark, by all accounts almost as boring as his wife. Anne had no interest whatsoever in *anything*. She was completely oblivious to the brilliant achievements going on all around her that were moving England into an age of greatness. London was awash with talent; a veritable tsunami of writers, artists, architects and philosophers had descended on the capital. Among the leading names of the day were Christopher Wren (still the most famous architect in the world), James Gibbs, who built St Martin's-in-the-Field, the philosophers Newton and Berkeley, the painters Kneller and Thimhill, essayists and poets such as Addison, Steele and Pope. One could go on and on but Anne failed to notice any of them. The fact that England was the most polished, civilised and sophisticated country on earth passed her by too. Possibly we can find a clue to her behaviour in her nickname, 'Brandy Nan', as she was callously called, referring to her love of the tipple. What little talents she may have possessed disappeared at the bottom of the bottle (to put this into perspective, it's along the lines of Queen Elizabeth II not noticing the 'swinging sixties').

In 1707 England and Scotland were formally united and in 1713 the Treaty of Utrecht was drawn up. On both occasions Queen Anne was bundled into St Paul's Cathedral to attend a service of thanksgiving seemingly oblivious to what was going on.

The only lasting impression Anne left on London was the development of Kensington Palace and, in particular, the gardens (technically, she also created Ascot races but the jury is still out on whether that's a good thing). Her apartments at KP were extended by the addition of several new rooms behind the King's Gallery. It was in the gardens, however, she left her mark that can still be seen today. The King, a keen gardener, had laid these out in the Dutch style but Queen Anne insisted on a formal French design. She enclosed 100 acres of Hyde Park as a deer paddock, laid out new gardens to the west and north stretching as far as Bayswater and built the Orangery, with its extremely fine architectural interior, designed by Hawksmoor and Vanbrugh.

The only love Anne had ever known was for Kensington Palace and the bottle. Ultimately, she died unhappy and alone. She was only 49. Having failed to produce an heir, she went to her death deeply concerned about the future of the monarchy. Her last words were reportedly, 'My brother, my poor brother,' referring to James II, long dead, whose son, The Old Pretender, was anxious to press his claim to the English throne.

Anne was buried at Westminster Abbey in a coffin that had to be virtually square in order to accommodate her vast bulk.

Unfortunately, The Old Pretender stayed nothing more than a wannabe and Anne was eventually succeeded by George I, Britain's worst ever king and, arguably, the finest argument for abolishing the monarchy ever produced. He made Ebenezer Scrooge look like the patron saint of Happiness. George hated everyone and everything. He hated England, he hated poetry, he hated paintings, he hated his wife, he hated his son and, just for good measure, he hated his daughter-in-law as well. Strangely enough, no one much cared for him either. He couldn't speak English and made no attempt to learn. German was the required language of George's court and anyone who couldn't speak it was treated with contempt (hardly unsurprisingly in an English royal palace, not many people *could* speak German and so French or Latin was used to communicate with the King). All in all, making George King of England seemed a bizarre choice.

When George first arrived in England, his appearance brought about reactions similar to those that greeted The Sex Pistols some 300 years later. The more diplomatic members of the Royal Court described his appearance as 'slightly weird'. Everyone else described him as stark staring mad. He had a strange complexion, receding chin, colourless eyes, a very loud German voice (German never being a language that lends itself to friendliness) and, extraordinarily, the only ginger-coloured wig in history.

As if all of that wasn't enough, he also came readily equipped with two of the most extraordinarily ugly mistresses ever seen, not only at court, but also in the country. A fat one, Sophia von Kielmansegg, who was (hardly surprisingly) nicknamed 'The Elephant', and a tall, thin one, Ermengarda Melusina von Schulenburg, who became known as 'The Maypole'.

Incredibly, these 'ugly sisters' were not just comic figures, they were also completely and incorrigibly corrupt. The King's mistresses viewed England as a conquered land, fat and rich for the picking. Having come from the relatively frugal court of Hanover, they acted like British MPs on expenses, immediately placing enormous orders for furniture, silver, china, carpets, and all kinds of food and wine. Kielmansegg, The Elephant, had a beer allowance of 16 gallons a month. So vast were their demands for food that each mistress was given a separate kitchen allowance of £3,000 a year. And even this wasn't enough; both demanded an extra allowance for the candles that were used when the King visited them at night.

It wasn't so much a case of the lunatics taking over the asylum as the animals taking over the zoo. George naturalised the two ladies and then hung titles around their necks. The Elephant became the Countess of Darlington, while The Maypole was given a series of Irish estates, making her Baroness of Dundalk, Countess and Marchioness of Dungannon, and Duchess of Munster.

Because of a few minor political problems across the sea, Irish rents were hard to collect, so she asked the King for a 'little something' in England as well. Thus, she became Baroness of Glastonbury, Countess of Faversham and, finally, Duchess of Kendal.

And, of course, with the title had to come jewels. The two mistresses took it upon themselves to 'raid' the late Queen Anne's apartments and go through all the drawers and cupboards in search of loot. They showed up at court the following day festooned in the royal jewels. So efficient were these two foragers that at George II's coronation his wife had to wear jewellery that her husband had rented for her; there was nothing left in the royal collection but a single string of pearls.

George I was deeply unpopular not just because of his boorish manners and preposterous mistresses, but also because of the fact that he kept his wife, Princess Sophia Dorothea, imprisoned at Ahlden Castle in Germany. Keeping one's wife in prison while openly flaunting one's mistresses was not considered cricket in the England of the early 18th century but, despite his deep unpopularity, religious bigotry was so severe that people still preferred an adulterous German Protestant idiot to that of a Catholic Jacobite.

However, every cloud has a silver lining and one great thing did result from the reign of George I – the idea that such an absurd man could become King simply through right of birth began to grate in people's minds, thus effecting a swing towards the power of Parliament, where the present incumbent, Robert Walpole was enjoying enormous popularity.

At the same time, Handel did a 'Madonna' and became the first contemporary pop star to settle in England, thus giving an immense impetus to British music.

When George I succeeded Queen Anne in 1714, he found Kensington Palace in a considerable state of disrepair and set about extensive rebuilding under the aegis of William Benson. By 1721, the original Jacobean house, the core of the Palace, had been completely replaced by three state rooms. Kent painted nearly all the ceilings of the Royal Apartments and was responsible for the *trompe-l'oeil* effect of the King's staircase. The north side of the house was filled by a self-contained residence, especially built for The Maypole. Eventually it passed to the King's grandson, Prince Frederick, thus receiving its present name, the Prince of Wales Court.

George I died on a visit back to Germany in 1727, and an English burial was never even considered – the country was glad to be rid of him. When German officials asked if the British wanted him sent home, they answered with typical British forthrightness: 'He *is* home!'

The next resident at Kensington Palace wasn't so easily forgotten. George II, though unpopular and extremely rude (inevitably, he was German), holds three unique distinctions within the history of the British Royal Family: he was the last English monarch to be born abroad (he was born at the Herrenhausen Palace in Hanover), he was the last reigning monarch to lead his troops into battle (against the French at the Battle of Dettingen) and he was the last king to be buried in Westminster Abbey.

These were some achievements for a man never born to be King of England ... or King of anywhere for that matter. He was 30 years old when his grotesque father was, somewhat improbably, invited to England to become its sovereign. After George I, England *should* have had a King Frederick. King

George II's eldest son, Frederick Louis, was expected to succeed
to the throne but, like many in those days, he died prematurely.
He was a keen player of the newly invented game of cricket and,
in the summer of 1748, he was hit hard on the chest by a cricket
ball while playing at his summer residence, Clivedon House, in
Buckinghamshire, and he died from his wounds in 1751. George
II hated him and, true to his character, wrote, 'I have lost my
eldest son, but was glad of it.'

Many people among the ever-tiring population of Great
Britain asked, what makes these people so mad? Is it just that
they are German? Certainly, in the case of George II, Freud
would have had a field day. By all accounts, he had an awful
childhood. Let's not forget, his ogre of a father had imprisoned
his mother when he was only 11 and it is doubtful he ever saw
her again (it is said that he did once try to swim the moat
surrounding the castle where his mother was imprisoned, but
failed to do so).

When his father was King of England, he would not allow
George to do the slightest of tasks or give him even the smallest
of responsibilities. Naturally, his resentment must have
smouldered and he and his wife Caroline of Ansbach, while they
were Prince and Princess of Wales, kept what was virtually a rival
royal court, in open contempt and defiance of his father.

It is, therefore, remarkable how well he did when he finally
came to the throne. His was a long reign, over 33 years, and
during that time, thanks to his able ministers and military
commanders, the strength and influence of England grew apace.

George threw himself into battle. At the age of 61, he led an
army of British soldiers (and German, Austrian and Dutch

mercenaries) to a conclusive victory over the French at the Battle of Dettingen. 'Don't tell me of danger,' he roared. 'Now, boys, fire and behave brave, and the damn Frenchies will run!'

And run they did.

In 1759, the year before he died, Britain was poised to achieve the greatest empire the world had ever known. England's military expansion, which he had overseen, led to massive conquests in Canada, India and the Caribbean, and the English Navy finally achieved complete mastery of the seas. Undoubtedly, George II had a successful reign but his successes were all the work of others and mostly a by-product of George I's disastrous period in office. It is ironic but, as the Empire increased, so the monarch's power lessened. The King was no autocrat (thank God, otherwise the Royal Family would have gone the way of the Romanovs a long time ago). Power was draining from the monarchy; the real wielders of control now were Walpole and Pitt, men of character and vitality, who envisaged a world dominated by Great Britain and who were already openly questioning whether there was a role for the Royal Family in the New World Order they were creating.

George II used Kensington Palace as his permanent residence and his wife, Queen Caroline, took much interest in the gardens and furniture. Charles Bridgman, the legendary royal gardener, landscaped the garden and William Kent added a revolving summerhouse. Another summerhouse, The Queen's Temple, became a park-keeper's lodge in the 19th century and was only restored to its original condition in 1976. During the 19th century, the gardens, already open to the public on Saturdays, became almost a public park, with the walls lowered or gradually replaced by small railings.

In the rounds is the Sunken Garden, opened in May 1909, adjoining the tree-lined avenue of Broad Walk. Here a statue of Queen Victoria, sculpted by her daughter Princess 'Louise', was erected by the residents of Kensington to celebrate the Golden Jubilee in 1887.

George II was the last reigning monarch to reside at Kensington Palace. But the ever-changing and large numbers of court passing through began to take their toll on the magnificent building. Towards the end of George's reign, half of the building was closed and much of it fell once more into disrepair. In the 19th century, the apartments were required for various members of the Royal Family and substantial alterations were carried out at a cost of £600,000.

In 1819, the Duke and Duchess of Kent were in residence and their daughter, Princess Victoria, was born in their apartments. Her christening took place in the Cupola Room. The Lord Chamberlain and the Archbishop of Canterbury brought the news of her accession to her at the Palace. Many had expected Queen Victoria to rule from either Kensington or St James's Palace and, indeed, she held her first privy council at Kensington Palace (on the very first day of her accession). However, almost immediately, she moved to Buckingham Palace and never again stayed in Kensington Palace.

Queen Victoria strenuously resisted suggestions that Kensington Palace should become the site of the National Gallery and instead installed royal relations in her inhabitable apartments. The Kents' apartments were occupied by the Duke and Duchess of Teck, and Queen Mary was born there in 1867. The Palace continued to deteriorate, however, and Parliament was persuaded to grant

£23,000 for its restoration on the condition that the state apartments were opened to the public. After careful restoration, they were officially opened on 24 May 1899, the Queen's 80th birthday.

Change continued throughout the early part of the 20th century. From 1912, the newly founded London Museum was housed in Kensington Palace until it was moved to Lancaster House in 1914, before being returned in 1951. After the state apartments were renovated in 1956, and again from 1972 to 1975 under the administration of the London Museum (which reopened in the Barbican as the Museum of London in 1976), they were then refurnished with more important paintings and furniture from the Royal Collection. The pictures now on display in the state apartments fall into two distinctive categories. There are, among the old masters, a series of royal portraits from the time of William and Mary, including the portrait of Peter the Great painted by Kneller when he visited the King in 1698, and a series of (principally 17th-century) continental pictures, including the ravishing *Cupid and Psyche* by Van Dyck.

During World War I, King George V allowed a number of rooms to be used by those working on behalf of Irish soldiers and prisoners-of-war. The Palace was used as the headquarters of the Number 34 Personal section during World War II and, in October 1940, incendiary bombs, and later a flying bomb, damaged part of the building. Prince Philip moved into the Palace during the 1930s and also stayed there in 1947, between his engagement and marriage. In 1955, Princess Marina, Duchess of Kent, Princess Alexandra and Prince Michael of Kent moved into the Palace. The use of Kensington Palace for the accommodation of royal relatives led King Edward VIII to describe it as the 'aunt heap'.

Diana at KP

The Prince and Princess of Wales moved into apartments 8 and 9 at Kensington Palace on return from their honeymoon in September 1981. For security reasons, their apartments were well out of the way on the Palace's north side. KP, as it was immediately christened by the press, became Diana's favourite home (years later, when the spoils of their marriage were being divided up by the lawyers, Diana insisted on being able to stay at KP). Charles and Diana's new home boasted rooms that were spacious and elegant, which Diana immediately called in Dudley Poplak to redesign. Poplak, an interior-decorator friend of her mother, was the dashing favourite of every Sloane that season. Charles is said to have held his head in mock anguish when he saw how the chintzy Sloane intended to transform the three floors of what was his home as well. The dominant colour was to be peach, which Charles dismissed as 'somewhat gay'. In vain, he pleaded with Diana to let David Hicks, the brilliant decorator married to Mountbatten's daughter Pamela, have the job. But Diana refused, declaring Hicks 'boring and predictable'. However, she did allow Charles to add a touch of class by bringing in furniture and pictures from the Royal Collections. The apartments' Georgian windows overlooked a private walled garden that Diana always referred to as her 'little oasis'. Access to this sanctuary was through a black door set in the surrounding brickwork. The garden was heavily scented with a multitude of different flowers (roses climbed halfway up the ten-foot-high walls) and such was the feeling of peacefulness that even such a cynic as Jeremy Paxman was moved to comment that it was hard to believe you were in the heart of London. During the blazing summer months, knowing no one else had access to the garden, Diana would sunbathe in the nude.

But not everywhere at KP was life so tranquil. As well as Charles and Diana, a veritable army of attendants and flunkies were ever present, including a full-time butler, housekeeper, valet, two chefs, two chauffeurs and a cleaner. Added to this were various members of the Prince and Princess's staff detailing that day's activities, a mass of equerries and two press officers. And, of course, the constant presence of two police protection officers awaiting their orders for the day.

Although Charles and Diana were the major stars at KP, they had a strong supporting cast; there were four other royal households based at the Palace, each one, in its own way, worthy of its own series. Gossip and tittle-tattle were the order of the day, as a network of informers kept their charges informed on who was doing what with whom.

Apartment 1a housed the then 51-year-old Princess Margaret, an ageing Mrs Stone living out her own Roman Spring. The Queen's fading, glamorous younger sister, who had been the 'Princess Diana' of her day, still maintained a glamorous lifestyle, despite her fading tan and the loss of her favourite toy-boy, Roddy Llewellyn. Margaret led a grand life; she hated to see daylight much before 11am, so always rose late. After a comfortable breakfast in bed, during which she would scan all the tabloids, she would go to her hairdressers, David and Joseph in Berkeley Street. If there were no other diversions available, she would attend a boozy lunch with one of her walkers at The Ritz.

When Diana first joined the Royal Family, Margaret, or Margo as she was known, befriended her, and they travelled together to royal events in Margaret's Rolls. But Princess Margaret was too seasoned a performer to allow Diana to upstage her. She would always exit the car first, letting the hosts know who the star was, and only then would she turn around and introduce Diana. It was always a canny move and certainly put the junior royal in her place, and let the assembled press now who was in charge.

Margaret was the first royal in history to understand the press and how to treat them. A product of the glamorous *la dolce vita* of the 1950s, she knew the power of the media. When her good friend the film director Bryan Forbes was fired as head of production at EMI's Elstree Studios, he thoughtfully phoned Princess Margaret to cancel a longstanding dinner date they had arranged for that day. Somewhat concerned that Forbes might be down in the dumps and in need of a friend, Margaret said, 'Why on earth would you want to do that?'

'Well, the press will be all over the place,' replied Forbes. 'You know what they're like.'

Margaret was having none of it. 'Darling! Just look down the lens and *smile*!' she responded gleefully.

But as Diana's star rose and Margaret's virtually went into free-fall, the two royal divas fell out. It all began when Diana fired her butler, Harold Brown. In his place, she promoted Paul Burrell. Immediately, Margaret picked up Brown for her own household, a move that incensed Diana. Well, aware that the Palace walls have ears, Diana's fortifications of her own world within KP did not include having a man who knew everything about her moving just along the terrace. Diana, far from being glad that her former employee had found a job elsewhere, threw an enormous tantrum and demanded that Brown get out of KP altogether – including his rent-free apartment. Somewhat out of her depth, Diana made the mistake of taking her argument straight into the enemy camp and confronting Margaret. The ensuing row ended with a wonderfully melodramatic Margaret shouting, 'Just remember who owns the flat … and who owns *yours* too.' Diana was flabbergasted. Margaret swept out of the room but it was no dignified exit stage left. She slammed the door so hard a framed print fell from the wall.

Diana's tantrum had been a big mistake and she knew it. Margaret was a formidable foe; not only did she have the Queen's ear, ringing her sister every day for a sisterly chinwag, but she enjoyed great relations with the network of flunkies so beloved of the Royal Family. Diana was acutely aware that she could do very little that wasn't immediately passed on to Margaret and stored for future use. And so, using various intermediaries, Diana held out an olive branch that Margaret accepted, albeit with some reluctance.

One useful legacy of this friendship was Diana's discovery that the approach to Margaret's front door in King's Court was the only one in the Palace not covered by CCTV (once upon a time Margaret had a juicy private life she wished to hide, although these days it was used as a convenient entrance by many of the employees). Better still, across the courtyard opposite Margaret's was a secret passage that led to the back entrance of the Waleses' apartment 8. Diana made full use of its secrecy. When the amorous Hasnat Khan was smuggled into the Palace courtyard under a blanket in the back of Diana's BMW, driven by Paul Burrell, the butler drove him not to the Princess of Wales's front entrance but into the unspoiled King's Court and the back entrance.

But by far the most enthralling relationship at KP was that between Diana and the occupant of apartment number 10, Princess Michael of Kent, who resided there with her husband, Prince Michael. Diana loathed both of them. The Kents were a throwback to a bygone age of royalty. Prince Michael, a bearded Tsar look-a-like, was the Queen's cousin and enjoyed a sumptuous lifestyle. Of his wife, Princess Michael, the Queen herself was moved to say, 'She is so much grander than us.' The jury is still out on whether Her Majesty was joking or not.

Princess Michael was a tabloid dream and it did not take Fleet Street's finest long to come up with the goods. When they did, it was such a great story that sometimes the old adage that God is a tabloid hack really does seem true. The *Daily Mirror* discovered her father had been a member of the SS. It was the Queen's Press Secretary, Michael Shea, who had the dubious honour of finding out if the story was true. After he confronted the Princess with the *Mirror*'s allegations, she said, according to Shea, 'I don't know. I will have to ask my mother.' Obviously, the question 'What did you do during the war, Daddy?' had never come up during Princess Michael's childhood. Princess Michael eventually called Shea back and said, 'It appears to be true.'

To be fair to Princess Michael's father, serving with Hitler's Panzer divisions during the invasion of Poland and Russia is hardly the subject for cosy family chats around the dinner table, but Diana relished the story, devouring all the tabloids and particularly enjoying Princess Michael being dubbed 'The Fuhrer' by virtually all of them. The nickname stuck and often Diana would enquire of her butler, Paul Burrell, 'What's the Fuhrer up to?' Whenever Princess Michael went for a walk in the KP garden, Diana would peer out of the window and say, 'The Waffen SS are on the march again.'

Convinced 'the Fuhrer' spied on her through the curtains, Diana would observe her through a pair of opera glasses. Diana also relished the open warfare between Margaret and Princess Michael too, going out of her way to court her friendship with Margaret along the classic lines of 'my enemy's enemy is my friend'.

Diplomatic relations between the two were finally severed forever after an incident involving a maid working for Princess Michael who had come to Diana in a distressed state. The maid had contracted breast cancer and claimed she had been dismissed shortly afterwards by Princess Michael. Diana asked the maid to relate the whole story into a tape recorder and then took the tape to one of her lawyers.

Princess Michael maintained that she herself had helped with the young girl's medical bills and that the maid herself had wanted to quit, thus giving up her grace-and-favour home. The young girl died of cancer three years later. Diana kept in touch with her right to the end.

Much further down the pecking order, and yet surprisingly well liked by the British public, were the 'other' Duke and Duchess of Kent. The Duke and Duchess of Gloucester and the Duke and Duchess of (confusingly, also named) Kent were lower-profile palace neighbours. In Mrs Thatcher's abrasive times, the writing was on the wall that these two ducal descendants of George V and their families were unlikely to hang on to their income from the civil list for long. The axe finally fell under Tory Prime Minister John Major in 1992, leaving them wholly dependent on the Queen's generosity. Hence, they never complained if the Queen's office dispatched them to open a Somalia community centre in Slough or a new motorway services on the M42.

The Gloucesters had a 35-room palace apartment, while the Duke and Duchess of Kent were ensconced at Wren House, inside the royal compound. 'Eddie' Kent is a strangely elongated version of Prince Charles, with whom he is close. He spends his time carrying out second-rate engagements that the big royals have passed on, while the Duchess has been known for her conversion to Catholicism. Diana came to see her as a sweet saintly woman whose charity work was an inspiration. She sometimes accompanied her on her hospital rounds and watched in admiration as the Duchess gave patients bed baths and emptied bedpans.

There was very little neighbourly interaction between the separate fiefdoms of Kensington Palace. Each had their respective private secretaries, equerries, ladies-in-waiting, butlers, chauffeurs, maids and valets (100 people in all, including Robert Fellowes and Diana's sister Jane, who had their own apartment inside the compound). The somewhat lukewarm friendship between Diana and Margo did not extend to the older woman ever inviting her to lunch, or vice versa. And relations with Princess Michael remained strained.

Like everyone else who has ever lived there, William and Harry loved KP. The two boys shared a cosy attic room that had been converted into a luxury nursery. The large comfortable room was painted a soft yellow. All of the furniture was hand painted with colourful animals and cartoon characters. The children's meals were served in the nursery and Diana would often join them, especially for afternoon tea.

Harry and William enjoyed their childhoods spent at Kensington Palace.

When the family spent the weekend at KP, both Charles and Diana would attend a special 'tea' that William would put on. Despite their marriage problems and eventual divorce, both Charles and Diana looked back on their days at KP as among the happiest of their lives.

☞ *Before entering the Palace main entrance, look for a black door in the wall.*

Black doorway

Using the black doorway hidden in the high wall that led from Princess Margaret's courtyard, Diana would slip through to take William and Harry to play at the children's playground at the north end of Kensington Gardens. This once small and very basic play area equipped with only a swing and a

William is pulled along by a friend's dog.

slide was originally at the location of the newly built Diana, Princess of Wales Memorial Playground.

The doorway became a regular secret exit for Diana, William and Harry in the early 1980s. As young toddlers, the Princes fed the ducks bread at the Round Pond each Saturday morning.

Diana would also sneak out alone through the door to rollerblade through the park's network of walkways and paths, the general public and paparazzi completely oblivious that the tall blonde in the baseball cap was, in fact, the Princess of Wales. More frequently, the Princess would join the throng of blading enthusiasts who were fast learning the new cool craze among the young and trendy. Every Sunday, the Broad Walk was littered with ad-hoc jumping ramps and overcoats laid out in makeshift slalom courses. Despite the temptation to be more adventurous aboard her skates, the Princess opted to concentrate on merely staying upright.

Diana spent many hours walking alone through London.

Diana was recognised by a group of young girls on one occasion and was promptly invited to join their synchronised gang, chatting happily as they gathered more speed and confidence.

After being photographed by a national tabloid newspaper leaving a late-night tryst with Hasnat Khan, in order to keep her then secret relationship with the doctor quiet, Diana offered a deal to the photographer. In exchange for the pressman's photographs of her, she would set up a far better set of photographs for him and his newspaper. Unknown at the time to the outside world, Diana revealed that she was a keen rollerblader and would gladly be photographed on them in Kensington Gardens. The photographer and his newspaper gladly agreed to hand over the film in return for a set of memorable photographs, which then appeared as a worldwide scoop. No mention of the secret deal was ever made public (see page 1 plate section).

☞ *Visit Kensington Palace via North public entrance.*

After your visit to Kensington Palace, turn right from the public entrance and retrace your steps, returning to Studio Gate on Palace Avenue, then stop at the main entrance security gates.

Freedom to roam

On 15 November 1993, during a speech at a luncheon in aid of Headway National Head Injuries Association, Princess Diana announced she was retiring from public life. She told a packed audience she no longer wanted to be in the public eye and that her life was sadly lacking any meaning. Although Diana's speech took everyone by surprise publicly, in private she had been telling friends and family for some time that she wanted out. Diana believed that she could lead a life like anyone else away from the glare of the public eye. In vain, her friends tried to tell her that this simply wasn't possible. She was easily the most famous woman in the world and also the most recognisable face on earth. The idea that Diana could lead a normal life was not only inconceivable to them, but also highly amusing. Diana, however, was a stubborn woman and, once she had an idea, she rarely let it go. To her friends' horror, she not only insisted her life would be normal from now on, but also that she would relinquish *all* police protection. At first, her friends thought she was kidding – how on earth could she expect to walk down a street unprotected? But Diana was convinced it could be done. Her only worries concerned the ever-present paparazzi but, she told her friends, she knew how to take care of them.

It was Sarah, the Duchess of York, who planted the seed of complete liberation in Diana's head; many years before, she had read W Somerset Maugham's *Theatre* and told Diana of a scene where the most famous actress in London goes out for a walk along Tottenham Court Road all alone. The actress is thrilled by the experience, especially when no one recognises her. Diana loved the story and Fergie convinced her that she, too, could do the same thing.

In some ways Fergie was right but in many ways she was wrong. Diana did manage to build something of a private life for herself but it was not in the way she had intended.

Diana did not always drive out of KP. Sometimes she would walk straight out of the main gates on an impulse and go wherever the mood took her. On one such occasion, in 1994, Diana, dressed in roll-neck sweater and casual trousers, tentatively walked out

Entrance to York House Place.

of the main gates at KP and down Palace Green until she arrived at York Passage, a small enclave just past the first security checkpoint. Diana walked through the passage, pausing to look at the construction work currently in progress on the buildings to the left. At the end of the small passageway, Diana skipped across Church Street and headed quietly into Holland Street.

Diana makes a quick escape into the back alleyways.

The Princess made her way to the boundaries of St Mary Abbott's Church, which stands hidden next to a small public garden.

☞ *Continue retracing your steps along Palace Green towards Kensington Palace Gardens (Kensington Palace Gardens is named Palace Green at this point). With Kensington Palace behind you, cross over Palace Green and go into the small alleyway that is adjacent, York House Place.*

☞ *Continue along the passageway until you reach a main road, Church Street. Cross over the road to the adjacent street, Holland Street. After approximately 40 metres, turn left into Kensington Church Walk. Follow the footpath to St Mary Abbott's Church and cloister on your left.*

Mary Abbott's Church

Diana stepped into the secluded courtyard of the church to answer a call on her mobile phone. She had recently taken charge of one of the new generation of mobile phones, much smaller and more compact than its predecessors, and she loved using it. Diana stayed seated on the small bench in the church graveyard for about ten minutes before snapping shut the phone and placing it away in her handbag.

She stood up and strode purposely as she continued her way through the small garden that leads on to Kensington High Street, stopping every few moments as she strolled to look in shop windows.

☞ *Continue through the small garden where you will arrive on to Kensington High Street. Turn right and walk 100 metres until you arrive at McDonald's on your right-hand side.*

Two Big Macs and fries

Diana was a frequent visitor to McDonald's in Kensington High Street, often taking William and Harry there. Dressed casually in jeans and a sweatshirt, with an American baseball cap perched on her head, Diana would queue with everyone else, looking at the menu above the counter and curtly informing Harry that, no, he could not have two big Macs *and* fries.

Diana always insisted that she wanted no special treatment and hated being offered the chance to jump the queue. On one occasion, Diana ticked off the manager, who offered to open a till that wasn't being used just for her. 'No, thank you, we'll queue like everybody else,' Diana said frostily, before adding, 'Why don't you open it for the other people who are waiting?'

☞ *Walk a further 50 metres. On the right you will find the location of WH Smith (now closed for business).*

The Great Escape

Eventually, the Princess arrived at WH Smith and went inside. She glanced around the shop to see if anyone had recognised her, then proceeded to the book section. Here she glanced through a copy of *OK!* magazine before opting to buy a copy of *Newsweek*. Diana then headed directly over to the entertainment and video section. As she peered along the lines of movies, she spotted *The Great Escape*. The World War II prisoner-of-war

Choosing a video in WH Smith for a quiet night in at Kensington Palace (see also page 2 of the plate section section).

film starring Steve McQueen was her father's favourite film. Still clutching the magazine in her hand, Diana grasped the copy from the shelf and read the blurb on the rear of the box. After glancing around, she then reached up to the top shelf and took down a copy of *Moby Dick* starring Gregory Peck and Orson Welles. Deep in thought and oblivious to others around her, the Princess was engrossed by the newly released video. After some time, she finally bought *The Great Escape*. Diana headed for the checkout queue and, while waiting to be served, craned her neck to read the headline of an Evening Standard newspaper that had been placed on the counter. The headline referred to her, as it frequently did so, and she smiled to herself as she read further down the page. The Princess took her time to get the correct money from her purse for the cashier, then headed outside with a satisfied smile. Although Diana had bought *The Great Escape*, the following day's headline in the *Sun* newspaper read: PRINCESS OF WHALES GETS MOBY DICK OUT! (see page 2 plate section).

☞ *Turn right and continue for 70 metres until you reach the junction with Phillimore Gardens. Turn right and 10 metres on your left is Sticky Fingers.*

Sticky Fingers

Sticky Fingers is a popular burger bar owned by ex-Rolling Stones bass guitarist Bill Wyman.

The eatery, tucked away in a corner of Phillimore Gardens was a favourite spot for Diana, as well as for her two sons, William and Harry.

Sadly, Prince Charles turned down the chance to eat there,

'It's the experience.' Diana meets Rolling Stone Bill Wyman in London.

otherwise a temporary reunion of the whole family may well have taken place in 1994. Prince William begged his father to come with them on a family outing but Charles wasn't a fan of either burgers or the Rolling Stones, preferring chicken salad and The Beatles.

Diana agreed with Charles about the burgers *and* The Beatles but told him, 'It isn't the food that matters … it's the experience.'

☞ *Return to Kensington High Street, turn right and continue in the same direction as before. The Non Stop Party Shop is 10 metres along on your right.*

The Non Stop Party Shop

Diana loved Kensington High Street and was never happier than when discovering a new shop. One such place was the Non Stop Party Shop, situated at the far end of the street towards

Giggling Diana offers no help to floundering butler Paul Burrell as she struggles to get party balloons in her car.
Top right and below
© Mark Saunders.

Holland Park. Thrilled with its massive collection of party treats and balloons, Diana was soon a regular customer. On one occasion, she attempted to fill her car with a mass of helium balloons, giggling like a schoolgirl as her butler, Paul Burrell, forced them into the vehicle, desperately trying to stop them all floating away.

☞ *Continue for a further 20 metres until you reach the black iron gates of Holland Park on your right.*

Holland Park

Diana would often jog through the grounds in the early hours. Other times she would walk through the park

Diana leaving Roberto Devorik's home and (right) *the grand gates at Holland Park.*

to visit her friend, Roberto Devorik, who had a magnificent residence on the far side.

☞ *Cross over Kensington High Street to the Odeon cinema on the opposite side of street.*

The Devil's Own

Diana regularly visited the Odeon cinema in Kensington High Street, frequently taking William and Harry to see an afternoon movie. On one occasion, she found herself in hot water when she took William and Harry to see the Brad Pitt movie *The Devil's Own*. The film, which co-starred Harrison Ford, was highly controversial due to its apparent sympathy for Brad Pitt's character, a former IRA hit man. In vain, Diana pleaded that she

had no idea the film portrayed
the IRA as little more than a
bunch of lovable rogues. She had
read reports that the film was a
thriller and, as both William and
Harry were Harrison Ford
fans, had thought it a perfectly
acceptable movie for them to
see. (Diana remained a Harrison
Ford fan to the end of her life,
and the last film she ever saw

The Odeon cinema on Kensington High Street.

was *Air Force One* at a private-screening room in Soho with Dodi
Fayed, two weeks before she died.)

Prince William and Diana cross Kensington High Street after watching The
Devil's Own *at the Odeon.*

☞ *Stay on this side of the street and head back along Kensington High Street. After approximately 200 metres, you will arrive at Boots, at the junction of Wrights Lane.*

Diana could often be seen driving along Kensington High Street in Prince Charles' open top Aston Martin (see page 64).

Window shopping

Boots the Chemist, in Kensington High Street, was a store Diana loved to walk around with no particular inclination to buy. Often she could be spotted wandering through the make-up aisles, her face a study of intent as she picked up this or that beauty product. She was a particular fan of bath oils, as a visitor to KP once commented, 'The bathroom was full of bath oils ... not particularly expensive or elaborate ones, the kind you could buy at any high-street store.'

The last time Diana was seen at Boots was three days before her final summer holiday in St Tropez with William and Harry. She bought a large tube of after-sun and, making use of the store's '2 for 1' offer on suncreams, a can of sunscreen especially developed for the protection of the eyes.

☞ *A further 40 metres on your right is Marks and Spencer.*

M&S

In 1995, during a trip to Moscow, Diana was speaking to a Russian diplomat's wife who told the Princess that her husband was being transferred to the Russian Embassy soon. She asked Diana where she could find the store of 'Mark and Spencer'. Diana giggled and told the woman, 'It's called Marks and Spencer and it's in Kensington High Street.'

'Is that far from the embassy?' the lady asked.

Diana, knowing the Russian Embassy was situated directly behind Kensington Palace, laughed again and said, 'Not far at all. Straight past our place and turn left.'

☞ *Continue 150 metres to the Palace Green Gates on the opposite side of street and to the left of the Royal Garden Hotel.*

The Palace Green Gates

The Palace Green Gates were known in royal circles as 'The Polo Exit'. Whenever the Princess headed west to Windsor or Cirencester polo clubs to watch Prince Charles and sometimes her lover James Hewitt play polo, she would leave by this gate.

Until recent terrorist atrocities in London, the gateway was unmanned and the public could drive their cars through to the Bayswater exit at the top end, although there were warning signs advising drivers that you shouldn't do so.

It was also the exit for Highgrove, the Gloucestershire home of Prince Charles and Princess Diana. The Prince would drive them through the gates in his Aston Martin, complete with the roof down, closely followed in a back-up car by their police protection officers, into Kensington High Street. The 100-mile journey would take them over an hour to finish but it would then take Diana two hours to set right her wind-blown golden hair.

☞ *Cross over the road and continue past the frontage of the Royal Garden Hotel to the King's Arms Gate.*

The Royal Garden Hotel

The Royal Garden Hotel is a five-star luxury address defined by its location. It's well worth a visit to the restaurant on the top floor, which commands incredible views of Kensington Palace, Hyde Park and the Royal Albert Hall.

Diana wasn't so keen on what could be seen from the hotel,

The Royal Garden Hotel offers exclusive panoramic views of Kensington Palace.

however, after it was pointed out to her that the rooftops of Kensington Palace were clearly visible to guests staying on the top floor. Diana had often gone up to the small roof garden to sunbathe during the long hot summers, discreetly pulling off her bikini top. She had never realised her private nude sunbathing was on such public display.

King's Arms Gate

Tucked into the end of a private road that runs alongside the magnificent Royal Garden Hotel, the King's Arms Gate is often missed by the hordes of tourists that visit Kensington Palace and its surrounding parks. And it's easy to see why. There are no signposts announcing its position. The gate stands almost anonymously, carefully watching the Kensington traffic while maintaining a discreet aloofness. And yet there was a time when Diana used this exit most days, discreetly nudging her car into the traffic on Kensington Road on her way towards either Mayfair or Knightsbridge.

In 1994, Diana was photographed driving through the King's Arms Gate for a late-night tryst with the then married Oliver Hoare seated next to her in the car (see page 2 plate section). (For a more detailed look at their relationship, please see Walk 2.)

☞ *Enter Kensington Gardens on your left just after the King's Arms Gate. Find your way to Palace Gate, keeping Kensington High Street (now Kensington Road) on your right-hand side.*

At Palace Gate, join the Diana, Princess of Wales Memorial Walk, which is marked on the ground by a plaque.

The Diana, Princess of Wales Memorial Walk

The Diana, Princess of Wales Memorial Walk meanders through several parks in London, including Kensington Gardens, St James's Park, Green Park and Hyde Park and, as well as a time for reflection about Diana, offers some of the greenest and most beautiful landscapes in the city.

Along the seven-mile route there are 89 plaques designed and sculpted by Alec Peever. The Memorial Walk was officially opened in June 2000 at a cost of £1.3 million. Controversially, no members of the Royal Family, including her sons Prince William and Prince Harry, were present at the opening.

The route passes a number of locations important to Diana's story: Kensington Palace, her home for 15 years; Buckingham Palace, where she lived after her engagement to Prince Charles

The Princess of Wales Memorial Walk is marked with plaques in the ground.

Prince Harry speeds along on his bicycle.

was announced; St James's Palace, where Prince William and Harry both have apartments; Clarence House, the former home of the Queen Mother; and Spencer House, the ancestral home of the Spencer Family.

☞ *After 500 metres, you will reach The Albert Memorial on your right and The Royal Albert Hall across Kensington Road.*

The Albert Memorial

Queen Victoria and her husband Albert shared one of the great loves of history, yet they rarely feature in the top-ten all-time great love affairs. They were unlucky in that they just didn't have star appeal, or a romantic image or any particular historical significance. Whatever the reason, Victoria and Albert never made it to the exalted ranks of Romeo and Juliet, Nicholas and Alexandra, Napoleon and Josephine, Anthony and Cleopatra, John and Yoko, or even David and Victoria. The reason for this is probably because they were just so boring. Although Queen Victoria remains one of the most loved and successful monarchs in history, she never really did anything except be a Queen. Oh, of course, the British Empire expanded throughout her reign and there were very few countries on earth that did not have a British ex-pat community complaining about something, but these achievements were all carried out by others; Queen Victoria herself never conquered anything, or discovered anything. Consequently, there are hardly any anecdotes or stories concerning Victoria and Albert that are worth retelling. And herein is their PR problem. To have a love of any historical significance and importance something has to happen. Tragedy always works: Romeo and Juliet, star-crossed lovers, dying in each other's arms; a last kiss and a farewell speech written by Shakespeare – perfect! David and Victoria, standing together and bravely facing the first wrinkle lines and grey hairs, knowing the onslaught of middle age will bring horror upon horror as cellulite, receding hairlines and reading glasses enter their perfect lives.

No matter how hard you try, Victoria and Albert just don't have these great stories. They met and married, like so many other royals, at the behest of others. Queen Victoria had always said she would never marry; she honestly believed she was married to her job and her position as sovereign was to be her full-time vocation. The powers that be, however, didn't see it this way. They wanted the Queen married for purely practical reasons. Queen Victoria was barely 20 years old when she became Queen of a powerful nation and head of the largest empire on earth. There was every possibility of a long reign ahead for the woman who only a short while before had been an immature, innocent Princess. She would need emotional and practical support in her new job that only a husband could provide.

Victoria, already beginning to feel a certain loneliness in her elevated position, relented and agreed with her advisers; maybe marriage wouldn't be such a bad idea after all. They now needed to find a man who would be quite prepared to take a subservient role to his wife, never question her judgement, and spend the rest of his life living in her shadow.

Of course, there were one or two other factors to consider. He couldn't be German; they had tried that one before and discovered that Germans make lousy English monarchs. The Danes and Swedes were out because they were such pifflingly small potatoes and had no money, the Americans were far too vulgar and didn't have a monarchy anyway, the French were vulgar and monarchless. And then there was the problem of Russia. Back in 1839, Tsar Nicholas was forever trying to expand his boundaries and had long had an eye on the English throne via a well-organised dynastic marriage. He had recently invaded Afghanistan and could promise to expand both Russia and Britain's Empires after his brief foray into the picturesque Afghan mountains north of the final frontier of the British Empire, India. The British tactfully ignored him, realising that anyone foolish enough to invade Afghanistan would be tied up in the godforsaken place for years.

There was also another matter the advisers were somewhat concerned about involving the young Queen. She had begun to suffer from what we now call emotional and physical stress, although in those days it was known as being lazy. It is true Victoria wasn't pulling her weight; instead she was putting it on … alarmingly fast. Victoria's weight gain appeared all the worse because she was so short. She tried to diet by drinking less beer and watching her calories, which, in the days before rehab, was considered a jolly sensible way to lose weight. But for Victoria life rapidly became intolerable. The colour of her hair was suddenly not to her liking; her clothes were all the wrong size (too small). She complained of headaches and feeling sick all the time. To combat these emotional mood swings, Victoria refused to wash or clean her teeth. And she told anyone who would listen she was depressed.

That the Queen might be suffering depression sent shockwaves throughout the court. She was, after all, the granddaughter of King George III, who was completely bonkers, and a careful watch was placed on Victoria for any signs of hereditary madness.

In 1839, Victoria's cousin Prince Albert of Saxe-Coburg visited London and she fell in love with him. Although he initially had doubts about the marriage, the couple were eventually married in February 1840. Victoria and Albert were married for 21 years, during which they had nine children. When he died of typhoid fever in December 1861, Victoria was heartbroken. She completely withdrew from the public view, spending her time grieving in the Scottish highlands Albert had so loved.

In tribute to her late husband, Victoria, who was born and raised at Kensington Palace, placed a memorial in the park, the most exuberant statue in the whole of London. It stands on the south side of Kensington Gardens, opposite the Royal Albert Hall. Before his death, the Prince told Victoria he did not want a statue as 'it would upset my equanimity to be permanently ridiculed and laughed at in effigy'.

The Albert Memorial was designed by Sir Gilbert Scott in 1872 and measures 180 feet from tip to toe. The whole thing is gilded gold and surrounded by 169 marble figures from history.

The Frieze of Parnassus, which runs around the base, features amorous poets, painters, sculptors, architects and composers. Above that are a group of virtues, angels and images representing the continents (Europe, America, Asia and Africa), arts and industries (agriculture, commerce, engineering and manufacturing).

The gold-leaf Prince was added three years after the unveiling. The original sculptor by Carlo Marochetti was turned down by Queen Victoria and he was still working on the second when he died. The third was built by JH Foley and completed by Thomas Brock in 1875.

Albert's name was to feature many years later on one of the strangest gifts ever presented to the Royal Family. The sumptuous yacht that had once belonged to Hermann Goering, Commander-in-chief of the Luftwaffe, was presented to the Royal Family by Field Marshal Montgomery. The yacht was named *Carin 2* in honour of Goering's first wife, who had died in 1931. The Royal Family rechristened her the *Royal Albert*. Following the birth of the Prince of Wales, she was renamed the *Prince Charles*.

In 1960, the Queen, possibly feeling it somewhat politically incorrect to own a yacht that had once belonged to the Nazis, returned the vessel to Goering's widow, his second wife, Emmy. Apparently, it was later used to host reunions of former members of the SS.

The Royal Albert Hall

The Royal Albert Hall is one of London's most treasured and distinctive buildings, and is instantly recognisable the world over. The hall was originally supposed to be called The Centre for Arts and Science but the name was changed by Queen Victoria when laying the original foundation stone as a dedication to her late and dearly loved husband, Prince Albert.

The hall was officially opened on 29 March 1871 and, although official records show it was proclaimed open by Queen Victoria, this is not the case. After a welcoming speech by Edward, Prince of Wales, the monarch was too overcome to speak, so the Prince himself had to announce, 'The Queen declares this hall is now open.'

The Albert Hall has played host to some of the most famous classical, operatic and ballet concerts ever held. And on 15 September 1963, The Beatles and the Rolling Stones appeared on the same bill.

Tantrum

The Albert Hall was the scene of one of Diana's most famous tantrums. Diana was an emotional person, which made her behaviour unpredictable to say the least, and the worst example of this occurred at the Festival of Remembrance in 1983.

This sombre and formal event, held to commemorate those who gave their lives in two world wars, is one of the occasions when the Royal Family is on duty to represent the nation.

Just before they were scheduled to leave their home at KP for the two-minute drive to the Royal Albert Hall, Diana informed Prince Charles that she did not want to go and that nothing he could say would make her change her mind. Charles's increasingly desperate pleadings only seemed to increase her temper. Finally, running out of time and patience, Charles left on his own, leaving his wife shouting abuse in his wake.

However, no sooner was he out of the door than Diana's tantrum subsided and she turned to her bewildered hairdresser, Kevin Shanley, and said, 'I'm exhausted but how can I let people down?'

The Queen and Prince Philip arrive at the Royal Albert Hall for the Festival of Remembrance in 1984.

James Hewitt – lover and riding instructor.

When he arrived at the Albert Hall, Charles had explained that his pregnant wife was not feeling well. His white lie was somewhat exposed when Diana rushed in a full 15 minutes after the Queen. Her Majesty was furious; this was considered an insult not only to the monarch, but to the memory of the dead as well (see page 1 plate section).

☞ *Continue along the Diana, Princess of Wales Memorial Walk for a further 400 metres until you reach the road, West Carriage Drive at Mount Gate. Cross over the road. In front of you is the horse-riding track. This side of the road is now called Hyde Park. Head right along the track or path to The Pavilion on New Ride.*

Major James Hewitt

Diana first met James Hewitt at St James's Palace in 1986. Hazel West, the celebrated wife of Lieutenant-Colonel George West, the Assistant-Comptroller in the Lord Chamberlain's Office, introduced the pair.

The party was held in two rooms in the West's spacious apartment at the Palace. It was an intimate gathering; no more than 20 people were present and Diana had come alone.

After they had been introduced, Hewitt reminded Diana they had met briefly before, at Buckingham Palace immediately after her wedding. Flirtatiously, Diana said, 'You look a lot better in uniform.'

The pair continued to talk. Diana, making no attempt to move among the other guests, told Hewitt she remembered seeing him play polo. Inevitably, the conversation moved on to the subject of horses as James Hewitt had given lessons to Princess Michael the previous summer.

After Diana's love affair with James Hewitt (right) *became public knowledge, Prince Charles* (left) *and his polo team were matched to play against each other at the Royal Berkshire Polo Club.*

Diana admitted to Hewitt she was terrified of horses. She had fallen off a pony and broken her arm when she was a child, after which she had sworn she would never ride a horse again.

Despite what people say about James Hewitt, he *is* a gentleman. Naturally concerned, and more than probably flattered that Diana was speaking to him, he explained that a bad fall off a horse in many ways resembled a car crash. 'If you don't get straight back into the vehicle, you'll never drive again,' he told her. 'It's the same with horses … you just have to get straight back on.'

Hewitt offered to help Diana overcome her fear. She looked

at him immediately and said, 'That would be wonderful. I'd love you to teach me. Could we go riding together?'

A couple of days later Hazel West, who was also one of Diana's Ladies-in-Waiting, telephoned Hewitt and asked again if it was possible for him to give the Princess riding lessons.

Crackling with excitement, hardly able to believe what was happening, Hewitt cleared it with his commanding officer at Knightsbridge Barracks and two days later stood proudly in the indoor riding school, welcoming his royal visitor.

In James Hewitt, Diana had found the perfect teacher. The fact that he also became the perfect lover was, at that time, an unexpected bonus. Within a couple of days, she had lost her fear of horses and the pair were enjoying the unimaginable beauty of Hyde Park first thing in the summer mornings.

They always took the same route: left out of the gates of the barracks towards Kensington Palace, along Rotten Row, through the glorious avenue of sycamores and chestnut trees that is the perfect location for horse riding. Hewitt never wore uniform, just a hacking jacket, tie, breeches and boots, with a trilby perched on his head. Diana, still not 100% sure of her horse-riding skills, always wore a hard hat, which had the effect of making her less noticeable.

In the late autumn, James Hewitt was posted to Comber-

Luciano Pavarotti and Diana meet after his performance in Hyde Park.

mere Barracks in Windsor and the early-morning rides ended. Although Diana never rode a horse in Hyde Park again, she did continue to walk the route on her own the following summer.

☞ *Retrace your steps to the road-crossing point and continue northwards along West Carriage Drive for 150 metres. After passing a car park on your right, turn right and continue down a path that leads to the Diana, Princess of Wales Memorial Fountain, which can now be seen in front of you.*

Diana, Princess of Wales Memorial Fountain

When the Diana, Princess of Wales Memorial Fountain was first opened, cynics dismissed it as a 'moat without a castle' and, with that unique pig-headedness only art critics can employ, it was considered little more than a meandering stream of solid concrete, with water running over numerous ruts and gullies.

But as you stand in front of the fountain just take one moment to listen, what do you hear? That's right ... the sound of children playing. And is there a greater memorial to Diana possible than a child's laughter?

The Queen opened this unique and beautiful memorial to Diana on 6 July 2004. The design of the fountain aims to reflect Diana's life; water flows from the highest point in two directions as it cascades, swirls and bubbles, before meeting in a calm pool at the bottom.

The water is constantly being refreshed and is drawn from London's water table. The memorial also symbolises Diana's quality and openness. There are three bridges where you can cross the water and go right to the heart of the fountain.

Despite initial setbacks, the Diana, Princess of Wales Memorial Fountain is a great place to enjoy a day out.

It's the perfect place to sit on the grass, take your shoes and socks off, get the picnic out and watch the children play.

☞ *Retrace your steps to up to West Carriage Drive, cross the road and enter Kensington Gardens. Once inside the gateway, veer left and walk towards the Serpentine Gallery. Turn right at the gallery and continue alongside the building. This is the location where Diana arrived in her dynamic cocktail dress.*

The Serpentine Gallery

The Serpentine Gallery, which sits within the perfect splendour of Kensington Gardens East, was the scene of Diana's most triumphant appearance, and arguably one of the most famous photographs ever.

The night of Wednesday, 29 June 1994 was a night to remember, for that was the night she took the world's breath

The Serpentine Gallery.

away in a black cocktail dress at the same time as her husband admitted adultery on TV.

The whole of Britain knew that Charles would be interviewed on television that evening by the author and broadcaster Jonathan Dimbleby. And the word on the street was that it was going to be a sensation.

An estimated 15 million people tuned in that night, but Diana was not one of them. She had read leaked reports that Charles would confess to adultery at some point during the two-hour-long interview. Rather than stay at home alone to watch the spectacular, Diana accepted an invitation to a gala banquet at the Serpentine Gallery. She was the gallery's patron, a close friend of its chairman Lord Palumbo and guest of the then newly appointed chairman of the Arts Council of England, Lord Gowrie.

Dressed to thrill, Diana arrives at the Serpentine Gallery in 1994.

Diana prepared for the engagement racked with nerves, half her mind constantly on the documentary, the other half on whether her chosen dress was suitable. Outside the gallery, the world's media was ready for her arrival, desperate to capture her reaction to the Dimbleby interview.

As Diana made her appearance that night in a breathtaking off-the-shoulder, above-the-knee, black chiffon Valentino dress, Dimbleby's interview was all but forgotten. Diana looked sensational. She dazzled the guests and wowed the press.

The photos that appeared on the front pages of the world's press the following morning showed Diana smiling, relaxed and confident. Experienced Fleet Street snappers shook their heads in amazement. They knew Diana was good ... but never before realised she was *this* good.

The following day's newspapers had Diana on the front page; the future King of England admitting adultery, a significant event in any country at any time, was relegated to the inside pages.

☞ *Look eastwards across the park and in the distance you will see the Round Pond and, behind it, Kensington Palace. Find your*

The Round Pond in Kensington Gardens.

The Queen Victoria statue at Kensington Palace.

way across the park towards a statue of Queen Victoria, which stands in front of Kensington Palace on The Broad Walk.

Queen Victoria statue

Outside Kensington Palace stands a statue of Queen Victoria sculpted by her daughter, Princess Louise, to celebrate 50 years of her mother's reign. Victoria was born in the apartments of the Duke and Duchess of Kent (now the North Drawing Room) and christened in the Cupola Room in 1819.

☞ *To find your way to the nearest underground station, Queensway, with Kensington Palace ahead of you turn right and walk northwards along The Broad Walk until you reach Black Lion Gate on Bayswater Road. The station is adjacent to you as you exit the park.*

Walk 1 visitor information

Kensington Palace

OPENING TIMES

1 March–31 October

Daily 10am–6pm

Shop and Orangery 10am–6pm

Last admission 5pm

1 November–28 February

Daily 10am–5pm

Shop and Orangery 10am–5pm

Last Admission 4pm

Closed 24–26 December inclusive

Highlights of your visit to Kensington Palace

Diana, fashion and style exhibition

The exhibition of 18 dresses features seven never before displayed at Kensington Palace. The dresses include an early evening dress by Regamus from 1978–79 and a little black dress from 1995 by Gianni Versace. Many of the dresses on display were designed by Diana's favourite couturier, Catherine Walker.

Queen Victoria's bedroom

This is the bedroom where Victoria spent the last night of her youth. When she was woken up at 6am on 20 June 1837, it was to be told that her uncle had died in the night and that she was now Queen Victoria. She was just 18. Victoria's mother, the Duchess of

Kent, was rather over-protective and, until Victoria became Queen, always spent the night in the same bedroom as her daughter.

The King's staircase

It was this way that the King and his visitors would enter his State Apartments. You'll run into the King's Court in the stairwell. The staircase walls and ceiling are painted with William Kent's vivid, life-sized portrayals of George I's court and its various characters.

Mary of Modena's bed

This fine bed of red and blue velvet is called the 'Warming Pan Bed' because tradition has it that this was the very bed in which Mary of Modena, wife of James II, gave birth in 1688. This event was highly controversial because it provided the Catholic King with an heir. His enemies claimed that, in fact, Mary's baby had miscarried, and that an impostor had been smuggled into the bed in a warming pan and planted upon the people as a false prince. This was one of the events leading to the so-called 'Glorious Revolution' in which James II was deposed from the throne. Although the bed has James II's cipher on the head cloth – which is appropriate – the bed has been much messed-around with and how much, if any of it, really belonged to the warming-pan incident is debatable. Good story though!

Court Mantua

This bizarre fashion for enormously wide dresses developed into a kind of uniform that all the ladies at the Georgian court were required to wear. Ludicrously impractical, the dresses were worn over whalebone hoops and weighed down with heavy silver thread.

Royal Ceremonial Dress Collection

Fine fabrics, sumptuous dresses and pretty wasp waists aside, fashion at court tells a story about the social history of high society.

Court fashion moved more slowly than fashion in the wider world and court dress gradually became a kind of archaic uniform. Visitors to Kensington can see fashion in court dress from the 18th and 20th centuries, including a look at how the beautiful dresses and magnificent uniforms were created.

The King's Gallery

The largest and longest of the state apartments at Kensington Palace, the King's Gallery looks pretty much as it was when decorated for King George I in 1727. The King's Gallery was used for displaying pictures as well as for exercise and it is dominated by a copy of Van Dyck's noble portrait of Charles I on horseback at its east end.

The dial positioned over the fireplace is still connected to a wind-vane on the roof so that the King could see which way the wind was blowing, where his navy was likely to be heading and when the posts were likely to arrive. Created for King William III, it is still (amazingly) in working order.

Sunken Garden

The beautiful Sunken Garden was planted in 1908, transforming part of the gardens occupied by potting sheds into a tranquil ornamental garden of classical proportions. It was modelled on a similar garden at Hampton Court Palace and celebrated a style of gardening seen in the 18th century.

The Last Debutantes

Kensington Palace takes visitors on a journey into the glamorous and alluring world of the debutante with a new exhibition marking the 50th anniversary of the last court presentations. Fashionable afternoon dresses and ballgowns, including stunning examples of couture by Christian Dior and Pierre Balmain, as well as accessories worn by some of the 'debs' during the final Season of 1958, are displayed in this multimedia exhibition, which tells their stories against the backdrop of dramatic social change that heralded the arrival of the 'swinging sixties'.

En route refreshments in Kensington Gardens

The Orangery Restaurant

Designed for Queen Anne in 1704, this was once the setting for lavish court entertainment. Now it is a tranquil restaurant where you can enjoy leisurely lunches and afternoon teas.

See opening times above.
Telephone: +44 (0)844 482 7777
www.hrp.org.uk

The Lido Café

Offering seasonal fresh food, breakfast, lunch and early evening dinner in the summer are all served with stunning views along the Serpentine and a large alfresco dining area.

Opening hours: 9am–8pm in the summer.
10am–4pm in the winter.

Telephone: +44 (0)207 706 7098
www.lidohydepark.com/eat.htm

Diana-related restaurants en route
Café Diana
Opening hours: 8am–10.30pm daily
Closed 25–26 December
Telephone: +44 (0)20 7792 9606

The Royal Garden Hotel
Two restaurants, the Min Jiang Chinese restaurant with stunning views over Kensington Palace and Kensington Gardens, and also The Park Terrace restaurant.
Telephone: +44 (0)207 361 1999
www.royalgardenhotel.co.uk

Bill Wyman's Sticky Fingers Café
This haven of great food and original rock memorabilia provides an enviable environment for eating, drinking and relaxing. The invaluable collection of Stones memorabilia is a real talking point for both Stones fans and anyone with a taste for rock heritage.
Telephone: +44 (0)207 938 5338
www.stickyfingers.co.uk

En-route public toilets
Palace Gate / Mount Gate / Diana, Princess of Wales Memorial Fountain / Black Lion Gate

WALK 2

THIS WALK INCLUDES:

Photographer attacked! / A look at Princess
Diana's first London apartment / The secret trysts
with boyfriends / Hasnat Khan – a woman has
found love / Love nests / Secret liaisons with
reporters / Lunches / Harrods
department store / Sloane Street shopping / Diana's
first place of employment.

Length – *3.5 miles or 5.4 km*
Time – *4 hours*
Underground – *Earls Court*
Bus routes – *74, 328, C1 and C3 go to
Earls Court underground*

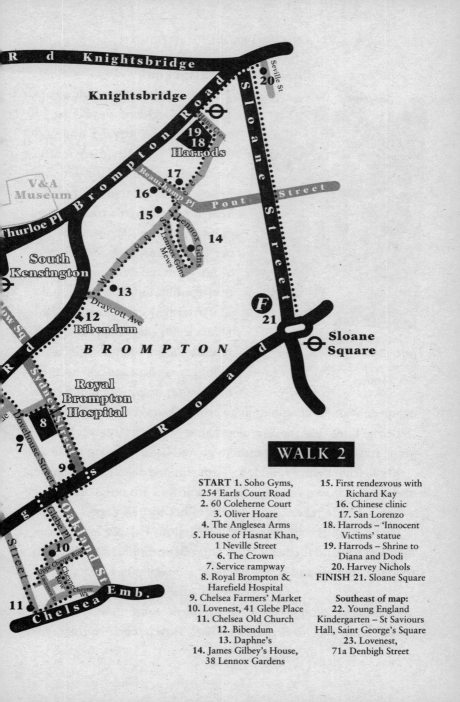

Knightsbridge

Knightsbridge

V&A Museum

Thurloe Pl

South Kensington

Harrods

Beauchamp Pl

Pont Street

Seville St

Sloane Street

Willow P

Lennox Gdns

Lennox Mews

Draycott Ave

Bibendum

BROMPTON

Royal Brompton Hospital

Sydney Street

Dovehouse Street

Glebe Pl

Upper Cheyne Row

Cheyne Row

Cheyne Wk

Chelsea Emb.

Chelsea

Oakland St

Street

Road

F 21

Sloane Square

WALK 2

START 1. Soho Gyms,
254 Earls Court Road
2. 60 Coleherne Court
3. Oliver Hoare
4. The Anglesea Arms
5. House of Hasnat Khan,
1 Neville Street
6. The Crown
7. Service rampway
8. Royal Brompton &
Harefield Hospital
9. Chelsea Farmers' Market
10. Lovenest, 41 Glebe Place
11. Chelsea Old Church
12. Bibendum
13. Daphne's
14. James Gilbey's House,
38 Lennox Gardens

15. First rendezvous with
Richard Kay
16. Chinese clinic
17. San Lorenzo
18. Harrods – 'Innocent
Victims' statue
19. Harrods – Shrine to
Diana and Dodi
20. Harvey Nichols
FINISH 21. Sloane Square

Southeast of map:
22. Young England
Kindergarten – St Saviours
Hall, Saint George's Square
23. Lovenest,
71a Denbigh Street

Photographer attacked!

Kevin Duggan taking film from photographer Brendan Beirne while Diana looks on.
Rex Features

In 1997, police were made aware of an incident involving a member of the Royal Family on the Earls Court Road. A scuffle broke out when award-winning Nikon Royal Photographer of the Year Brendan Beirne took photographs of Princess Diana as she left her Earls Court gym. Beirne was ordered by the Princess to hand over the film but he refused to do so. Passer-by Kevin Duggan asked Diana if he could help her. Diana replied, 'Yes, I want his film.'

Duggan proceeded as ordered by Diana, then pinned Beirne against a wall, holding him in an arm lock and twisting his wrist.

Beirne later told the *Sun* newspaper, 'I was frightened he was going to break it. I let the camera go and heard it being opened.'

Mr Beirne, then 39, added, 'I am stunned she did not step in and stop it. It was outrageous. She knows I am not a stalker or a threat. I have taken photographs of her for ten years.'

Diana took the film back to Kensington Palace. Any parties involved took no further action. Later Beirne and Duggan agreed to make amends and shake hands at a meeting in London.

☞ *Continue along Earls Court Road until you reach the crossroads with Old Brompton Road. Turn left and continue for*

50 metres along Old Brompton Road. The entranceway to 60 Coleherne Court is opposite the Brompton Library.

Coleherne Court

Entrance to 60 Coleherne Court.

Coleherne Court was Diana's first home away from her family. Her sister Sarah, then working for Savills, a leading London estate agent, found what was to become, for a time, the most famous address in Britain.

The three-bedroomed apartment in a mansion block at 60, Coleherne Court was Diana's coming-of-age present from her parents.

In July 1979, she moved into the £50,000 apartment and immediately set to work furnishing the rooms in a warm but simple habitat style. The white walls were repainted in pastel shades, the sitting room became pale primrose yellow while the bathroom was bright with red cherry.

Diana had always promised her schoolfriend Carolyn Pride a room when she got her own apartment. She was as good as her word. Sophie Kimball and Philippa Coaker stayed for a while but in August Diana and Carolyn were joined by Anne Bolton, who also worked for Savills, and Virginia Pittman, the oldest member of the quartet. It was these three who stayed with her throughout her romance with Prince Charles.

Diana looked back on those days at Coleherne Court as the happiest time of her life. It was juvenile, innocent, uncomplicated and, above all, fun. 'I laughed my head off there,' she said and the only black cloud was when the apartment was burgled and she had most of her jewellery stolen.

As landlady, she charged the others £18 a week and organised the cleaning rotas. Naturally, she had the largest room, complete with double bed. So that no one would forget her status, the words CHIEF CHICK were emblazoned on her bedroom door. 'She always had the rubber gloves on as she clucked about the place,' recalled Carolyn. 'But it was her house and, when it is your own, you are incredibly proud of it.'

At least she never had to worry about washing piles of dirty dishes and cups. The girls rarely cooked in spite of the fact that Virginia and Diana had completed expensive Cordon Bleu courses. Diana's two specialities were chocolate roulades and Russian borscht soup, which friends asked her to make and deliver to their apartments. Usually the girls devoured the food before it left Coleherne Court. Otherwise they lived on Harvest Crunch bran cereal and chocolate. 'We stayed remarkably plump,' observed Carolyn.

The house-proud teenager was also tidying up her career. Shortly after moving into her apartment, she found a job where she truly was in her element. For several afternoons a week, she went to work at the Young England Kindergarten run by Victoria Wilson and Kay Seth-Smith in St Saviours Church Hall in Pimlico. She taught the children painting and drawing, and danced and joined in the games they devised. Victoria and Kay were so impressed with her rapport with the children that they asked her to work in the mornings as well. On Tuesdays and Thursdays, she looked after Patrick Robinson, the son of an American oil executive, work that she 'adored'.

There were still loose ends in her working week so her sister Sarah took it upon herself to tie them up, employing Diana as a cleaner at her house in Elm Park Lane, Chelsea.

Diana leaves her flat to go shopping in 1980.

Sarah's flatmate, Lucinda Craig Harvey, recalled, 'Diana hero-worshipped her but Sarah treated her like a doormat. She told me not to be embarrassed about asking Diana to do the washing up and so on.'

Diana, who did the vacuuming, dusting, ironing and washing, was paid £1 an hour and took a quiet satisfaction in her labours.

When she became engaged to Prince Charles, Diana referred to her cleaning job in her reply to Lucinda's letter of congratulations, 'Gone are the days of jif and dusters. Oh dear, will I ever see them again?'

☞ *Next take the road, The Little Boltons, which runs down the left-hand side of Coleherne Court. After 250 metres, turn left into Tregunter Road, then walk another 50 metres. On the left is the home of Oliver Hoare at number 6.*

The bookshop

Despite the obvious pain Diana felt about giving up her public life, evident in her desperate attempt to hold back the tears following her announcement at the Hilton, she discovered a tremendous excitement had entered her world. For the first time in her life, Diana was completely free. Gone were the petty restraints of royalty, where even the simple act of using the bathroom became a constitutional exercise, and gone too were the even more excessive restraints of close protection. Diana had found security suffocating and, at times, exhausting. Like most people, Diana had her own idiosyncratic ways but, whereas the average person can do what they want, alone in their car, Diana always had a close police protection officer sitting next to her. It was difficult for Diana to sing in the car, or hurl verbal abuse at a radio talk-show host while a man sat next to her, discreetly looking out of the window and pretending he wasn't hearing anything. Diana also found it impossible to talk on the phone, especially as she always had the nagging doubt that whatever she was saying was being reported back to her husband. It was, therefore, with an incredible feeling of joy and excitement that she embraced her newfound world of freedom. 'Now I can be me,' she told close friends, holding her head above her arms and shimmering like a go-go dancer.

After the initial surge of adrenalin had settled down, Diana found herself nervously peering around her new world. It was all very well having the freedom to go anywhere and do anything she wanted … but where, exactly, did she *want* to go? And what was it she wanted to do when she got there?

The first thing she did was read, vociferously; Diana was well aware that outside the cosseted luxury of Kensington Palace a new world was emerging. London had once again gained the cultural high ground and 'Cool Britannia' was on the front page of *Time*. Diana, still barely in her thirties, wanted to be part of this world. She had always been a great reader; as a young girl she had devoured the novels of her step-grandmother, Barbara Cartland, often reading long into the night at Spencer House, her family's ancestral home. Diana would never dream of going on holiday without a book, the joy of sunbathing, which she loved, richly enhanced with a good read. But, despite the joy reading gave her, Diana was aware that her reading habits were of limited scope. She began to find trashy novels boring, preferring to read those books that stimulated her mind. Diana was always the first to agree her education had been limited. She once described herself to a journalist as 'thick as a plank'. In Diana's day, a young girl's education was merely an exhausting chore, something that had to be endured until one could find a suitable husband and raise a family. Five years at a private boarding school, rounded off by a year at a Swiss finishing school were the most education Diana ever received. But now, suddenly, she found herself desperate for knowledge. It had always been something of an agony when Diana had been forced to join her husband at private dinner parties. Prince Charles loved nothing better than to surround himself with intellectuals, men and women who were quite prepared to challenge his views on anything from architecture (on which he had many) to the current decline of the British theatre. For Diana, these conversations were an endurance, at times unbearable. She had no idea whom or what they were talking about. Contrary to popular opinion, Charles had tried to help her, recommending a long list of books she might try to read. Unfortunately, Charles made the quite common mistake of recommending books *he* found interesting, but which were well beyond the grasp of a young woman whose literary education ended at Mills and Boons.

Now, alone at Kensington Palace, Diana discovered a thirst for knowledge she had hitherto never felt. Like so many people, she began to think that education was carried out the wrong way round. As children, we just want to leave school and become an adult; once we are adults, we want to go back to childhood. To paraphrase King Louis XVI, 'As a young man I had strength, in my old age I have wisdom. If it could have been the other way round, I would have conquered many worlds.'

Diana's intellectual capacity was limited but she wasn't stupid. Like most of us, she probably could not have debated Quantum physics with Stephen Hawking but, around the dinner tables these days, she found she had a voice and opinions she wanted to air. During the first Gulf War, she had been glued to Sky News; her lover, James Hewitt, was in the Gulf and Diana was anxious to hear the latest developments from Kuwait. Now, Diana found 24-hour news strangely addictive. Her new life was taking her away from the day-to-day royal existence of opening hospitals and planting trees, and she was being courted by organisations such as the Red Cross. If Diana was to commit herself, she determined, it would be a hands-on experience. She no longer wanted to rely on press briefings to inform her of what to say and who to say it too. Diana wanted her own opinions, her own say. If the Red Cross was in Rwanda, she wanted to know *why* they were there and exactly what they were doing. And Diana was already hearing rumblings of the horror of landmines, a politically sensitive issue considering Britain's involvement in the arms trade.

With all of this intellectual enlightenment, Diana found herself bored by her old friends. She yearned for thrilling and exciting company. It depressed her that Paul Burrell was the only person she had to talk to. But then, just as Diana began to despair of finding the elusive thing she was searching for, Oliver Hoare came into her life.

And nothing was ever the same again.

The Boltons

Diana met Oliver Hoare in the early 1990s, just as her marriage collapsed amid much anger and suspicion, and it is supremely ironic that it was Diana's hatred and jealousy of Camilla Parker Bowles that brought the couple together. Oliver

Oliver Hoare was always the perfect gentleman.

Hoare had been drafted in to act as a go-between for a possible Wales reconciliation. Diana, recognising Hoare as a good friend of both Charles and Camilla, cannily figured this would put her inside the enemy camp.

It was through his wife, whose mother was a friend of the Queen Mother, that Oliver Hoare first met Charles and Diana at a party at Windsor Castle and, because of their shared interest in Islamic art and eastern mysticism, he and

First meeting: Oliver Hoare and Diana at Guards Polo Club after attending Ascot races in 1986.

Charles became friends. This was at a time when Diana was dismissive about her husband's esoteric interests and she placed Oliver Hoare firmly in the 'old and boring' category. With delicious irony, considering Diana was to fall in love with him, Oliver Hoare's mother-in-law lent Charles her mansion in France to carry on his illicit affair with Camilla Parker Bowles.

Oliver Hoare was 16 years Diana's senior and an established expert in obscure subjects about which Diana knew absolutely nothing and in which she had never expressed the slightest interest, but, if he was prepared to help to try to save the marriage, and give inside info about Charles and Camilla, Diana was quite prepared to talk to him.

To begin with, Diana was interested only in knowing what the other side was up to but, in the company of the suave, handsome ex-Etonian Hoare, Diana began to feel the first stirrings of romance. Oliver Hoare, with his boyish good looks and tousled hair, was fantasy in the living flesh. He was cultured, well read, intellectual and *very* good looking. Diana was well aware of his reputation as a ladies man; that was obvious to see in the way he handled his drink and through the flirtatious eyes that Diana could not look into without going weak at the knees.

Dazzled by Oliver Hoare's looks, Diana also found herself fascinated by everything he said. As well as being deeply intellectual, he moved in cosmopolitan and cultured circles that fascinated Diana. His friends included the late Russian ballet dancer Rudolph Nureyev, which elevated him to almost heroic status in her eyes. Forgetting his original role as a fifth columnist, Diana became genuinely interested in Islamic art. She asked him to recommend further reading on the subject and Hoare obliged, sending round a dozen books on its origins. Diana avidly read the books, discovering, through its art, the rise of Islam and how, at one time, it had been vastly superior to the western world. She read of glorious cities like Constantinople, Baghdad and Medina, which were hitherto little more than items on the evening news.

It was all interesting stuff; any westerner discovering Islam for the first time comes across a veritable Pandora's box of interest and Diana found it fascinating. However, her own fascination with the subject was not the only reason Diana wanted to learn everything about Islamic art.

She had fallen madly in love with Oliver Hoare.

Oliver Hoare had first 'come out' into London society as the protégé of a rich Iranian lady called Hamoush Azodi-Bowler who lived in considerable splendour in the painter Augustus John's old studio in Chelsea. She had taken Oliver with her to Tehran where he became interested in Islamic art and Sufism, a mystic branch of that faith. Once back in London, he became head of the Islamic department of Christie's auction house. In 1976, he married Diane de Waldner, the heiress to a French oil fortune, and started up as a dealer in Oriental art with his own shop in Belgravia.

Among the titled gentry and rich socialites that now frequented his shop, Oliver Hoare found himself in a world he had always dreamed of. His father, a civil servant, had scraped together enough money to send him to Eton, the finest letter of introduction in any meeting of society. Now his father's sacrifice was paying off: Oliver Hoare was as cool as a Tunisian sunset, his voice full of honey and his smile as laidback as an Eton cricket match in the middle of summer.

Whether Diana was unlucky with men or unlucky in love is a

matter of conjecture. There are only four men that we know for sure she loved, despite the claims of any number of tawdry paperbacks: Prince Charles, James Hewitt, Oliver Hoare and Hasnat Khan, of whom more later. Everything about her marriage to Prince Charles has been so well documented, both officially and unofficially, it seems pointless to go into it, suffice to say that Charles was Diana's first love and, as the father of her children, the most important love of her life. Despite evidence to the contrary, Charles and Diana made a determined effort to have a successful marriage but it ended in divorce like 50% of all marriages in Britain today. Ultimately, the marriage of Charles and Diana was a triumph, for William and Harry have turned out to be such remarkably likeable and astute young men.

Oliver Hoare was Diana's 'movie' romance. He was the moment when every emotion this emotionally charged woman had ever felt came crashing down on her head and set her off on a collision course that could only end in tears. He was the fantasy love affair that every woman, even married women, are allowed.

Like most people, when Diana fell in love, she became deaf, dumb and blind to reality. That she fell in love with a married man like Oliver Hoare, no matter how gorgeous, is a measure of that blindness. Diana wanted love, Diana *needed* love, but she had already played the ultimate fantasy love story: the little girl who found her Prince. Now she would be moving into that other area, so beloved of filmmakers and writers – unrequited love.

Oliver Hoare was enigmatic, well mannered, stylish and generous to a fault, and Diana was thrilled when he presented her with a couple of antique bracelets and a Persian rug. At the start of their affair, in the summer of 1991, Diana and Hoare would frequent those established restaurants, such as San Lorenzo, that Diana had always been seen in. They aroused no suspicion; Diana was often seen at San Lorenzo with male friends, as she told a journalist herself. What the waiting pack of paps didn't realise was that, often after eating at the restaurant, Diana and Hoare would discreetly move on to the Knightsbridge apartment of Mara Berni, the owner of San Lorenzo, in Walton Street, where their affair progressed rapidly. Such was Diana's love for Hoare that she had no qualms about taking him back to Kensington Palace, smuggling him in via the courtyard of Princess Margaret's apartment. Diana became a frequent visitor to Hoare's art gallery in Pimlico, calling in at least twice a week. She even celebrated her 30th birthday there, enjoying a cake Hoare had bought specially for the occasion with the staff. Diana and Hoare would also meet at Lucia Flecha De Lima's home at the Brazilian Embassy in Mount Street, sometimes staying there for a whole weekend together.

Despite the ongoing battles with her husband, and still maintaining a seething hatred of Camilla, Diana discovered a sort of happiness with Hoare. Like any sexually active woman, she wanted to look her best and so, in the spring of 1993, she started to frequent the Harbour Club in Chelsea. Hoare also joined and it gave them yet another public venue to meet without any undue suspicion arising. Diana took an interest in all aspects of Hoare's life and visited his mother Irina. After Hoare had talked to Diana about Sufism, a mythical branch of Islam he found particularly fascinating, she purchased a number of books on the subject, and, during her annual ski trip with William and Harry to Lech, in Austria, Diana was spotted on the balcony of her hotel, deeply engrossed in a book.

'What's she reading?' a television producer asked his cameraman.

The cameraman, Mike Lloyd, peered down his lens. 'Eh … *Discovering Islam.*'

The assembled journalists, hands cupped around steaming coffee, guffawed. The television producer laughed and said, 'What's she *really* reading?'

'She's *really* reading *Discovering Islam.*'

Hoare introduced Diana to a world she had craved: a world of intellectual simulation, art, books, history. *Everything* she had loathed about Prince Charles and his intellectual clique, she now embraced with Hoare. It was frightening the speed at which this new world engulfed her. Diana herself felt she had wasted so many years; she realised she had travelled the world and met everyone she ever wanted to meet, yet she didn't feel she knew anyone or anything. Oliver Hoare changed all that.

Diana visibly changed as a person too. She was in love and she was happy. She blossomed into beauty and she had time for everyone.

Unfortunately, however, this brave and exciting new world was about to come crashing down all around her. As Shakespeare once wrote, love is a wonderful, terrible thing, and for Diana that end was to bring about one of the most dramatic and embarrassing experiences of her life.

Diana seemed to be under the illusion that Hoare was preparing to leave his wife and move in with her. She had even discussed the possibility of moving to Italy with him. But, like so much else in Diana's life, this was simply a pipe dream. An impossibility that was never going to happen. Despite his affair with Diana, Hoare *was* happily married with three teenage children and he had an extremely successful career.

Inevitably, Diana began to suffer the bane of every mistress's life – jealousy. She found, despite her love for Hoare, she had no claims on him and every time he left her he went back to the arms of his wife. Diana's delusion became almost pathetic. She really believed Hoare was prepared to leave his wife for her but nothing could be further from the truth. Despite Diana's pleading, Hoare told her, in no uncertain terms, it was never going to happen. Instead of ending the affair there and then, Diana continued to see him, believing, as so many others have before, she could lure him away with her love. But again, Diana was living in a fool's paradise. It all became too much for her and eventually her jealousy destroyed the affair. Diana hated what she saw as Hoare cheating on *her* with his wife, and, inevitably, this jealousy turned to mistrust. She began to call him on his phone, demanding to know where he was. On one occasion, she followed him from his shop and discovered he was not going where he had told her. Diana confronted him on the telephone and accused him of seeing another woman. In vain, Hoare protested that he had simply changed his plans. 'I changed my mind,' he said in exasperation. 'Do I have to call you every time I change my mind?'

On another occasion, Diana jumped out of Hoare's car in the middle of Sloane Street, oblivious to the rush-hour traffic, because she suspected he was going to see his wife rather than, as he had told her, his sick daughter.

Eventually, inevitably, Hoare was forced to bring the affair to an end. Diana's demands were simply too great for a married man to live up to. He told her during a candlelit dinner at KP that it was all over. Diana was distraught. In another ironic twist that seemed to be the hallmark of Diana's life, one of her best friends echoed the very words Ken Wharfe had spoken to a hapless James Hewitt when Diana ended *their* affair: 'It is over. Live with it.'

But Diana couldn't live with it. Inside she was seething. She felt she had been used. The anger burned inside her like a fire. She couldn't sleep at night, couldn't eat, even her daily trip to the gym had become something she loathed. Everywhere she looked she saw reminders of love lost. Diana was suffering as only those who have truly loved can suffer.

Inevitably, Diana's anger turned to hate and dangerous thoughts began to play on her mind. She began to create impossible scenarios, that all she had to do to win back Hoare was to remind him she was still around. In the finest traditions of the 'bunny boiler', the mistrust that had replaced jealousy was now replaced by cruelty. She took to phoning Hoare at all hours, sometimes up to 30 times a day, using the landline at KP, her mobile, even the telephone box at Beltan Place, just around the corner from the Harbour Club. In desperation, he pleaded with her to stop but Diana was a woman scorned. She felt, as she had felt so many times in her life before, that she had been treated badly, not seeming to realise that this time most of the fault lay with her. She also took to driving around Hoare's house in the middle of the night and staring up at the windows, her own imagination conjuring up images of Hoare and his wife tucked up in bed. The phone calls continued, and now Diana began to call him at his house. If Mrs Hoare answered the phone, Diana would hang up and then instantly ring back.

In a desperate attempt to stop the nuisance calls, Hoare agreed to meet Diana at the Harbour Club. Diana was about to make the same mistake that she had made a million, a billion, a *trillion* times before. She intended to plead with him, to say that she would take him on *his* say, that she would do anything he wanted if he would just please continue to see her. But she was saved from making a fool of herself, as he didn't show up. Diana was incensed. Throwing caution to the wind, she drove straight from the Harbour Club to Tregunter Road and banged on Hoare's door.

There was no answer; Hoare sat alone inside the house listening to the almost animal-like howling from a clearly distressed Diana. Eventually, she went back to her car and cried her eyes out.

Diana's behaviour left Hoare with no choice but to call in the police. His wife had demanded he do so after their children became frightened by the calls in the middle of the night. Hoare stalled; he had been badly shaken by Diana's presence at his front door but he knew what a scandal it would be if the news of Diana's antics were leaked to the press. In a diplomatic attempt to avoid the law, Hoare had approached Prince Charles but was told there was very little Charles's camp could do. If Diana were to deny making the calls, it would look for all the world as if Charles and his people were ganging up on her again.

The matter was reported to the police and a special bug was installed in the Hoares' telephone. It did not take long to discover where the phone calls were coming from. They were traced to Diana's landline at Kensington Palace and her mobile phone, and some were traced to several public telephone boxes in the

Kensington area. Later, when the story leaked, Diana's good friend and confidant Richard Kay, a *Daily Mail* journalist, attempted to rubbish the claims by suggesting Diana was at the hairdressers when some of the calls were supposed to have been made. It did not take the press long to find out there was a phone box just around the corner from Diana's hairdresser.

The story broke, like so many stories before, in the *News of the World*, in August 1994. The paper's royal reporter, Clive Goodman, splashed details of the 'cranky' calls across the front page and revealed the police investigation had pinpointed Kensington Palace as the source.

Diana had been told the paper was intending to run the story the previous week, when she had been on holiday in Martha's Vineyard, America, and had received a tip from an ex-protection officer. Although it's unlikely the *News of the World* will ever reveal their sources, the ex-cop told Diana, 'It's someone close to home.'

Diana was in despair. She flew back from America not only with the knowledge of the ensuing scandal in her mind, but also with the ominous words of the ex-detective hanging dangerously in the air: 'Someone close to home.'

Like so many who have faced adversity, Diana found herself strangely cool headed. She needed a plan and she needed it fast. She couldn't stop the *News of the World* publishing; apart from anything else, she *knew* she had made the calls and any attempt to take legal action and force an injunction would be folly. The very best she could hope for from the courts would be a one-week stay of execution but the evidence gathered by the newspaper was so irrefutable that the *News of the World* would not only win on appeal, but have a million dollars' worth of free advertising as well.

Diana sat alone at Kensington Palace, considering her limited options. 'Someone close to home...' She pondered those words again, going through a list of suspects that invariably drew a blank. Her source was impeccable, she knew that, and also a man with a foot in both her camp and Charles's. She knew for sure the leak had not come from Charles's side – they simply did not play that way. What happened in Diana's life affected William and Harry; neither Prince Charles nor any of his people would do anything so utterly out of character as to tip off the *News of the World*.

Eventually, Diana came up with a plan. It was risky but a risk she had to take. The *News of the World* would be publishing the story on Sunday. That meant the other newspapers and the wire services would pick it up early Sunday morning. There was no doubt it was a massive story that would be front-page news all over the world. What Diana needed to do very quickly was to rubbish the story herself. Even if some papers did not believe her, she could still plant enough doubt in people's minds to enable her to crawl out of the wreckage. The intense rivalry between Britain's newspapers, especially the tabloids, was the key.

The Royal Family had long had an ostrich-type approach to scandalous stories printed about them. 'Never explain, never complain,' was their somewhat bombastic attitude to the press. To some extent, this approach worked. As long as a story stayed this side of libel, what difference did it make if it was printed? Republicanism had not been a major political force for over fifty years; if tabloid readers enjoyed a little bit of royal scandal alongside their daily dose of tits and bums, who cared? Commenting on what were in many cases completely fabricated stories would merely serve to give credibility to the tale.

But Diana was somewhat more media savvy than that. She had watched in horror as the tabloids destroyed her good friend the Duchess of York after photos were published of her having her toes sucked in the South of France. The royals' traditional approach of 'Never explain, never complain' was fine for *them*, safely cosseted behind the walls of Buckingham Palace. Fergie had been thrown to the wolves and her carcass hung up for all to see.

Diana was determined this was not going to happen to her. Potentially, making nuisance and highly illegal phone calls was far more scandalous than a bit of toe sucking. To beat this rap, Diana's plan would need to be cunning, savvy and brilliant. And in order for it to work she would have to enlist the help of the very people she was fighting. Diana was going to take the fight right into the middle of the enemy camp; metaphorically, she was going to explode a grenade in the heart of Fleet Street.

That she thought of it at all is a tribute to her media savviness. That she managed to pull it off was a work of genius.

Diana knew Sunday was a lost cause; the *News of the World* had its cake and would eat it in front of everyone. The other Sunday papers would take what crumbs they could and bake their own cakes. The only damage limitation Diana could do would be to keep quiet.

Monday was an all together different matter, however. Traditionally, Monday is the slowest news day of the week. If there has been no big splash in the Sunday papers to follow up,

Monday is invariably a time for an 'is there life of Mars?' type of story. But this Monday, Diana knew there would be a *massive* follow-up. The moment the *News of the World* hit the streets, journalists would be roused from their beds or the drinking dens of London and ordered to get to work on the follow-up.

Diana's plan was to pre-empt that follow-up. In the light of no official response from the Palace, there would be very little to do in Fleet Street except reiterate the *News of the World*'s story. Of course, any number of 'friends' and 'close pals' would be quoted but essentially the story would remain the same.

Diana intended to kill the story *in her own words*. She would be the first royal to go on the record since the Edward VIII abdication speech. She knew, of course, it would never be allowed; that the Palace would positively forbid her, as an active and senior member of the Royal Family, to do anything so tacky as speak 'on the record' to a tabloid newspaper.

But Diana had been in the spotlight for too many years. She had long ago shown an instinctive grasp of what the press wants and she was about to use all her knowledge to her benefit. Showing cunning beyond belief, Diana telephoned *Daily Mail* journalist Richard Kay early on Saturday morning and told him about the news story that was about to explode across the pages of the *News of the World* the following day. Diana said she wanted to get her side of the story out but, of course, as a journalist, he would understand she could not give an official interview. Would it be possible for Kay to conduct an interview with her and then attribute the words she spoke to a 'close friend'? That way, Diana would get her story out without embarrassing the Royal Family. Kay, of course, agreed, well aware she was giving him an absolute belter of a tale. Surprisingly, rather than have him come to Kensington Palace, Diana asked if they could meet in a small square in North London. Naturally, Kay agreed; he would have travelled to the dark side of the moon if it meant an exclusive interview with Diana, albeit one that was to be attributed to her 'friend', in what would be one of the biggest news stories of the year.

As Diana pulled out of Kensington Palace early that Saturday morning, the checkpoint Charlie just outside the main gate radioed ahead to the second checkpoint Charlie by the main exit. 'Fifty-two rolling,' they said and, as the words travelled across the airwaves to be picked up by anyone who just happened to have their radio scanners tuned into 99mhz, three members of the ever-vigilant ever-waiting paparazzi put down their coffee, extinguished their cigarettes and started their motors.

As Diana pulled into the traffic on Kensington High Street and drove towards Park Lane, the three paps slipped in behind her. It was just after 11am. Across the city, behind the still barbed-wire fences of Fortress Wapping, home to the *Sun* and the *News of the World*, the first editorial conference of the day was just starting. (For the conclusion of this story, please see Richard Kay and Talbot Place on p169.)

☞ *Continue to the end of the road, then turn right into Gilston Road. At the T-junction, turn left. You are now in Fulham Road. Walk for 450 metres and turn left into Elm Place. Fifty metres and past the right-hand bend is The Anglesea Arms on the left.*

The Anglesea Arms.

The Anglesea Arms pub

The Anglesea Arms pub, on Selwood Terrace, was Hasnat Khan's local. Apart from the obvious attraction of its proximity to both his flat in Neville Street and Brompton Hospital, Hasnat loved the place because of its unbearably romantic atmosphere. On several occasions during the summer of 1996, he came here with Diana and they sat on tables outside enjoying the cool evening together.

☞ *Turn left past the pub into Selwood Terrace, then turn right into Onslow Gardens after 10 metres. Turn right into Neville Street. At the bottom left-hand end of Neville Street is the doorway to number 1.*

1 Neville Street

The small basement flat at Number 1 Neville Street is where Hasnat Khan lived … and it is here that Diana found true happiness.

Diana *loved* Hasnat Khan, of that there is no doubt, and when people describe her life as 'tragic', that she never married him is surely one of the biggest tragedies at all.

The couple met at the Royal Brompton Hospital in the autumn of 1995. Khan, a heart surgeon, was working under the auspices of the distinguished surgeon Professor Sir Magdi Yacoub. Diana had gone to visit a friend who was critically ill, and, as she sat by her friend's bedside, Dr Khan, surrounded by a retinue of assistants, entered the room. He took no notice of Diana; like most professional doctors, he was more interested in the patient he was treating. But, if he ignored Diana, the same certainly could not be said for Diana's reaction to the doctor. She was so mesmerised by the handsome 36-year-old that her jaw literally dropped. It was a good job Diana did not have to get up to shake hands as her knees were so wobbly she doubted they would hold her up.

Some people just *know* when they have found 'the one'. As Hasnat Khan swept from the room, his assistants in tow, Diana knew that moment had arrived. She was in love and, unlike Oliver Hoare, the last man she had loved, Hasnat Khan was single.

For Diana, it was as if a brisk 'tally ho' had been sounded. She immediately laid siege to Fortress Khan or, more precisely, the Royal Brompton Hospital; she made *19* consecutive daily visits, always making sure she showed up at a time Doctor Khan would be in attendance.

Diana pursued him with her usual *modus operandi*. She went

Diana was in love with Hasnat Khan. On his way to work at the Royal Brompton Hospital from his flat in Neville Street.

out of her way to learn all about him, suddenly becoming as keen a student of cardiology as she had been of Islamic art. She read *Gray's Anatomy* and studied surgical reports, and it did not take long to get what she wanted. In the autumn of 1995, just two years before her death, Diana was at her physical and sexual peak. The long hours in the gym, the sensible diets and the thrill and exhilaration of being free had created a woman few men could resist, and it did not take long for Hasnat Khan to succumb to her charms.

Although there was never a formal announcement, the couple started dating in October 1995. To begin with, they would meet at the hospital, Diana's role as a 'Queen of people's hearts' the perfect cover. For some reason, Diana and hospitals just seemed to go together, so it was barely mentioned in the press when Diana was routinely seen coming out of the Royal Brompton Hospital. As the affair progressed, they took to spending nights in Khan's small apartment in Neville Street, a slightly more salubrious address than the image of a council flat conjured up at the inquest into Princess Diana's death.

For Diana, the flat spelled domestic bliss. It was everything she had ever wanted. What some people could not, and probably never will, grasp is that Diana was not looking for wealth. She could get that anyway. Diana wanted love and, for Diana, love had no value, it was not something you put a price on.

☞ *Continue in the same direction to rejoin the Fulham Road, turning left at the end of the street. After about 100 metres, Dovehouse Street can be seen on the right. Walk over the zebra crossing and into Dovehouse Street, where The Crown can be seen on the right.*

The Crown Pub is now a restaurant.

Nights out at The Crown

By the summer of 1997, Diana and Hasnat Khan were involved in a full relationship. One night, when he was working at the Brompton Hospital, they managed to slip out for a quick drink at the nearby Crown pub.

The Crown is a cosy little local with only a very small space around the bar and a quiet dining area at the rear. As Hasnat brought the drinks, Diana, dressed ultra-casual in jacket and jeans, with a baseball cap pulled down over her hair, played the fruit machine that was tucked just inside the door.

Carrying the drinks, Hasnat came behind her and watched briefly as she fed the machine.

Fortunately, Diana's gambling career came to an abrupt halt when she glanced out of the window and spotted a paparazzo

Diana drinks a beer.

just getting off his motorbike. Hastily, the couple moved to the rear of the pub where they sat at a dining table to finish their drinks. In order to avoid having their photograph taken together, they left separately after about 30 minutes.

Diana's love for the enigmatic and handsome doctor continued unabated. She sometimes disappeared for a whole day to Khan's flat, where she contentedly vacuumed, did the dishes and ironed his shirts – reprising her old days with the jif and dusters. On the night of her birthday, she reportedly went out to meet Khan wearing her best sapphire and diamond earrings and a fur coat with nothing underneath.

Paul Burrell helped run the affair behind the scenes. If they had a lover's tiff, he would deliver a message to The Crown where Khan was hanging out. Diana was practised at keeping things secret, and the press rarely found out about the men she was seeing if she didn't want them to.

She made trips to Pakistan when she could to bone up on Hasnat's heritage. Her new best friend was Jemima Khan, the beautiful 22-year-old daughter of Annabel and James Goldsmith, who was married to Pakistan cricket legend Imran Khan. The two women sat up talking late into the night about how to handle marriage to a traditional-minded Muslim. Diana even asked Paul Burrell to talk to a priest about the possibility of a secret marriage to Dr Khan, and the butler had a meeting with Father Tony Parsons at the Roman Catholic Carmelite Church in Kensington High Street, where Burrell's son was an altar boy. The priest told him it was impossible to marry a couple without notifying the authorities – or, perhaps more importantly, without having notified the fiancé. Hasnat Khan was aghast when he learned of Burrell's consultation and said to Diana, 'Do you honestly think you can just bring a priest and get married?'

Eventually, the strain of the relationship became too great for Hasnat Khan and he ended it during an emotional meeting at Battersea Park. Diana pleaded with him not to finish but Khan's mind was made up. Under pressure from his own family to find a Muslim wife, the last man that Diana ever truly loved walked away and left her in tears.

☞ *Carry on to the end of the road and turn left at the T-junction. The road bends right. After 20 metres, you will see Cale Street on the left. Walk along Cale Street 10 metres and at this point on your right you can see the service ramp at the rear of the Royal Brompton and Harefield Hospital.*

Martin Stenning.

Brompton Hospital

Diana was quite used to being pursued by the press. She regarded them as an irritating fact of life, but one 'pseudo' paparazzo, Martin Stenning, went too far and forced Diana to take legal action against him.

Diana's relationship with the press was volatile to say the least but she did appear to understand they were doing a job, and she used or manipulated the press herself when it was to her

*On the look-out for Stenning.
Diana leaves the Royal Brompton
after meeting Hasnat Khan.*

benefit. In many ways, Diana's relationship with the press could be described as Faustian, the ultimate pact with the devil.

The snappers that followed her and the reporters that wrote about her were professionals, many of them award-winning veterans of Fleet Street. These men and women had press cards vetted by the police, NUJ cards and worked for, or on behalf of, the biggest, most powerful news agencies in the world. But, although no one can deny Martin Stenning the right to make a living as a paparazzo, he had had no professional training, no experience and no one to pull him back if he went too far.

In a sworn affidavit, Diana, giving her address as Kensington Palace, London W8, claimed she was extremely threatened and intimidated by Stenning's behaviour. She described Stenning as looking very grubby, unlike most of the photographers she saw.

From early 1996, Diana claimed Stenning repeatedly followed her on his motorcycle, which she said he rode 'aggressively, and dangerously close to my car'.

In a sworn affidavit, seen by the authors of this book, Diana lists a number of further encounters, many of which, Diana claims, reduced her to tears. On one occasion, a visit to her lawyers in Southampton Row left her 'shaking'.

Stenning's constant hounding, Diana claimed, was like a recurring nightmare. The affidavit lists encounters with Stenning all over London, including one at the Royal Brompton Hospital on 10 June 1996, during which Diana ran up a ramp to confront Stenning. After she got back in her car, she claimed she drove past Stenning, who was standing on a street corner laughing at her with his hands in the air. Diana said, 'He seemed to be enjoying taunting me.'

Eventually, Diana could take no more and she instructed her lawyers to find some way to stop the intolerable harassment.

On 16 August 1996, a court order, issued in the High Court, London, was granted, which banned Stenning from coming within 300 metres of Diana and prevented him from communicating with her. At the time of her death, Stenning was still trying to get the injunction lifted.

☞ *Continue along Cale Street and turn right at the end into Sydney Street. Walk down the right-hand side of Sydney Street for 250 metres, where you will arrive at the Chelsea Farmer's Market. Just through the entrance, the café is located on the left-hand side of the walkway.*

Hasnat forgets his wallet and lets Diana pay for coffee.

Chelsea Farmer's Market

During the inquest into Princess Diana's death, Mohammed Al Fayed dismissed her relationship with Hasnat Khan by saying, 'How could a man who lives in a council flat take care of a princess?'

Al Fayed had certainly inundated Diana with gifts – bracelets, watches and a ring – and she had access to all of the Al Fayed paraphernalia of helicopters, yachts and staff.

When Diana wanted to visit a clairvoyant in the West Country, the Harrods helicopter was laid on for her; when Dodi wanted to take her out for a romantic meal, a Lear jet flew them to Paris for the evening.

It seems Mohammed Al Fayed made it clear to Dodi that, while he was romancing the Princess, money was no object.

It is, therefore, terribly endearing and actually highly amusing that, during a visit to a small café in Chelsea Farmer's Market with Hasnat Khan, Diana was forced to search her handbag for cash to pay for the two cups of coffee and a Danish when Hasnat discovered he had not brought his wallet.

☞ *Continue in the same direction along Sydney Street to the T-junction at King's Road. Turn right along the King's Road and after 100 metres cross over the road into Glebe Place. You are now entering one of the most beautiful areas of London. Walk to the end of Glebe Place where it bends right, then further bends to the left. Number 41 can be found on the left-hand side of the street.*

Love nest

Diana and Oliver Hoare enjoyed trysts at a number of different locations during their affair. But by far Diana's favourite was Glebe Place, a small avenue tucked discreetly behind London's famous Cheyne Walk.

Secret Trysts: 41 Glebe Place.

Hoare had borrowed the spacious, three-bedroomed ground-floor apartment from a friend, and he and Diana enjoyed many romantic nights here together.

On one memorable occasion, Diana and Hoare had arranged to have a romantic evening meal

Oliver Hoare.

here but, to Hoare's horror, discovered they had no wine to go with the simple pasta dish they had prepared together. Diana quickly jumped into her car and went to the Wine Cellar on nearby King's Road. She returned to the apartment red faced and empty handed, for, despite still being married to the future King of England, she had discovered she had no money in her handbag.

☞ *Follow Glebe Place to the end and turn right at the T-junction into Upper Cheyne Row. After 10 metres, follow the road as it turns left into Lawrence Street. Then 40 metres on the right, walk down the alleyway, Justice Walk. At the end, turn left into Old Church Street. At the end is Chelsea Old Church on the left.*

Chelsea Old Church

Princess Diana attended the wedding of her former flatmate Carolyn Pride to William Bartholomew at Chelsea Old Church on 3 September 1982. Carolyn was more than a friend to Diana, she was a soul mate. From the time they shared the innocent days of Coleherne Court together until Diana's tragic death, the pair remained friends. Carolyn is Prince Harry's Godmother and, to this day, she remains in contact with him, taking delight in

Beautiful in pink, Diana attends a wedding.

his achievements, knowing how proud Diana would have been of him.

Carolyn helped Diana through some of her darkest moments. Indeed, it was Carolyn who insisted the Princess get help for the bulimia that was destroying her life in the early 1980s. And Carolyn was one of the friends who spoke at length to Andrew Morton prior to the publication of *Diana: Her True Story*, the groundbreaking biography that

Flat mate Carolyn Pride gets married at Chelsea Old Church.

lifted the lid on Diana's marriage to Prince Charles and very nearly toppled the Royal Family. After the book was serialised in the Sunday Times, in June 1992, Diana made sure photographers were on hand when she visited Carolyn at her Fulham home. The visit was made to let people know that Carolyn had spoken with Diana's approval and that everything she had said was true.

☞ *Take the path that runs down the right-hand side of the church that leads to Cheyne Walk.*

Cheyne Walk

Behind every door of these tall elegant houses there is a story to tell. Since the 18th century, Cheyne Walk has attracted famous people from all walks of life.

At the small crescent that heralds the start of this famous street, Bram Stoker, the creator of Dracula, lived at number 27. Next door, the footballer George Best had a flat years later. In 1718, John Salter opened his world-famous coffee house Don Saltero's at number 18, while the famous Italian composer Rossetti lived next door but one, at number 16, with a number of exotic animals. Sir Paul Getty, the billionaire philanthropist, took over the house in the 1980s.

But the most intriguing address must be number 3, where Rolling Stone Keith Richards and his then girlfriend Anita Pallenberg lived. The bedroom in which they slept was used in the movie *Performance*, starring fellow Stone Mick Jagger. In later years, Richards looked back on his time at Cheyne Walk with tremendous fondness. 'We never needed an alarm clock,' he said. 'The drugs squad would always wake us promptly at 6am every day.'

Richards added, 'We saw Diana when we played Wembley in 1997. She came backstage to see us. She was so beautiful. I remember so clearly when she left, she walked to the door, turned and said, "That was such a great show," and then she went.'

☞ *Continue along Cheyne Walk into Cheyne Row on the left. At the end, turn right into Upper Cheyne Row and continue to the end of the street. Turn left into Oakley Street. At the end of Oakley Street, turn right into King's Road, then left, and back into Sydney Street.*

In love and without a care

Sydney Street is where Diana was happiest. Every time she left the Royal Brompton Hospital and Hasnat Khan, she would skip along the road like a teenager in love. Startled members of the paparazzi would be greeted with a cheery 'Good afternoon' as she made her way to her car, always parked on a meter, without a care in the world.

On one memorable occasion, she stopped and chatted to some builders, hard at work. They suddenly found themselves in conversation with one of the most famous people in the world.

Chatting to the builders in Sydney Street (see also page 3 of the plate section).

☞ *Walk to the end of Sydney Street to the T-junction with Fulham Road. Turn right and continue along Fulham Road for approximately 200 metres.*

A man to trust

Graham Smith was one of Diana's first protection officers and a man she trusted implicitly. They met on board the royal yacht Britannia during Diana's honeymoon cruise with Prince Charles. Despite being somewhat older than Diana, she found him a man she could talk to and he eventually became something of a father figure. It was Smith who told Diana not to be daunted by her husband's intellectual table talk. Instead, he encouraged her to be more open and be prepared to offer criticism if she felt it was needed.

Diana contrived to have Smith transferred to the protection officers stationed at Highgrove, arguing quite sincerely that, as she had to have security around her all the time, it would be easier being shadowed by somebody she admired and could talk to.

Sadly, Graham Smith died of cancer in 1993. Towards the end of his life, Diana spent every day at the hospital with him. Touchingly, she apologised for making his life hell during his time with her. After rows with Charles, Diana would storm off in her car and spend the night driving around the countryside on her own. It meant a great deal to her when, just before he died, Smith said that he would not have changed anything in his life ... especially the time he spent with her (see page 3 plate section).

☞ *Bibendum is on the right.*

Bibendum.

Bibendum

Diana always maintained that the exclusive (and highly priced) Bibendum restaurant was the best place in London to watch the world go by. Situated smack bang in the middle of Sloane Ranger territory, Bibendum's unique open frontage gives guests an *al fresco* impression but protection from the elements means that it's a perfect all-year-round venue.

Like most Chelsea residents, Diana always referred to Bibendum as 'her local'. She was a regular diner throughout the summer months and once took her lover Hasnat Khan there for lunch. The couple had been intending to go to nearby Daphne's but got scared off when they saw paparazzi photographers loitering outside. The men were waiting for Annabel Goldsmith, one of Diana's closest

friends, and had no idea that the
mobile-phone call Annabel took
during her meal was from Diana,
literally just around the corner.

Hardened royal hacks always
maintained Bibendum was Diana's
favourite venue for making *de
facto* public statements.

On 18 October 1985, Diana's
most formidable rival Camilla
Parker Bowles stole all of
Diana's limelight by attending a
high-profile party at The Ritz
Hotel. Showing off her slightly

...beautiful, carefree and relaxed.

trimmed-down figure in a stunning black gown, a radiant
Camilla beamed at photographers.

To the amazement of the paparazzi, 15 minutes later Prince
Charles turned up. The party was for mutual friend Lady Sarah
Keswick but the joint appearance of Charles and Camilla was
highly significant.

The following day's press was full of photos and stories about
Charles and Camilla. Was this the woman who would replace
Diana? Fleet Street asked.

Diana was well aware of what was going on. Charles and
Camilla would be seen more and more together, and eventually
the public would look on them as a couple.

Diana acted quickly. At lunchtime the following day, she went
to Bibendum and made sure the paparazzi got pictures. Looking
beautiful, carefree and relaxed, Diana gave out her own message.

Top left: Princess Diana in Majorca, Spain, in 1987.

Top right: Rollerblading in May 1996. *News International*

Bottom left: Paul Burrell battles helium balloons outside Kensington's Non-Stop Party Shop in 1994. *Rex Features*

Bottom right: A pensive Princess Diana at Remembrance Day in 1984.

Above: Buying a movie in the WH Smith in Kensington High Street, 1995.

Below: Making a getaway with Oliver Hoare.

Top left: As Diana attended a *Vanity Fair* party in June 1994, Prince Charles was confessing to adultery.

Top right: Princess Diana on Sydney Street near the Royal Brompton Hospital where Hasnet Khan worked.

Bottom left: A 1984 shopping trip accompanied by trusted protection officer Graham Smith.

Bottom right: Diana on a London street with the pager she came to favour over mobiles.

Top left: On the way for a secret meeting with *Daily Mail* reporter Richard Kay in April 1994.

Top right: Paul McCartney and Diana in Lille in 1992

Bottom left: Prince William arrives for his first day at nursery in Notting Hill...

Bottom right: ...and Harry leaves Whetherby after dropping off his brother.

Above: Princess Diana on Beauchamp Place in 1994.

Below: Back in 1982, Lady Diana Spencer worked for a kindergarten in Pimlico.

Top left: Paul Burrell accompanies the Princess on a visit to hairdresser Daniel Galvin.

Top right: Following a rugby accident at school in 1996, William had to go to the dentist.

Bottom left: Diana frequently had appointments in Harley Street.

Bottom right: An appointment at the Hale Clinic in 1994.

Top left: Raine Spencer lived in Mayfair in 1996.

Top right: In Hong Kong.

Bottom left: Lunch with Sarah Ferguson in Mayfair in 1995.

Bottom right: Competing in William's sports day in the summer of 1989.

Above left: It was the Queen Mother's birthday in August 1988 at Clarence House.

Above right: Ascot in 1987 with Sarah Ferguson.

Bottom: Will Carling and Diana.

'I couldn't care less about them,' she said and, as the press photos of Camilla were already being wrapped around the first fish and chips of the day, Diana was back on the front page. In the war of the Waleses, Charles and Camilla would never beat Diana in a photo opportunity.

☞ *Continue along Fulham Road a further 100 metres and turn right into Draycott Avenue. After 30 metres, keep right, passing through the no-entry signs and Daphne's is on the left.*

Daphne's (left). William van Straubenzee kisses Diana during lunch date at Daphne's (right). Rex Features

Daphne's and William Van Straubenzee

The ultra-expensive Daphne's was opened 40 years ago by theatre agent Daphne Rye, and this historic venue was the favoured meeting place of Diana and her close friend William Van Straubenzee.

Van Straubenzee, an ex-boyfriend of Diana's elder sister Sarah, was clean cut, well bred, reliable, unpretentious and good company … everything Diana loved in a man. The fact that he was an ex of Sarah elevated Van Straubenzee considerably in Diana's eyes.

As a young girl newly arrived in London, Diana used to iron Van Straubenzee's shirts prior to his dates with her sister, and there is no doubt she developed quite a crush on him.

In 1993, Diana spent the weekend with Van Straubenzee at Floors Castle, the Scottish home of the Duke and Duchess of Roxburghe. Unfortunately, it wasn't the wonderful weekend Diana had been hoping for. Van Straubenzee was spotted when he arrived at Heathrow Airport for the flight north and Diana's dream of an idyllic break suddenly collapsed in ruins. The couple were also spotted playing tennis together at the castle, famous as the scene of Prince Andrew's marriage proposal to Fergie. For Diana, who maintained Van Straubenzee was 'just a good friend', this was the moment she realised she would never be able to be seen with a man, no matter how innocent, without the press speculating on the relationship.

When they got back to London, in despair, Diana arranged for Van Straubenzee to accompany her to her favourite restaurant, San Lorenzo. This time she made sure the snappers were waiting and, after alighting from the car some way up the street, she walked alongside Van Straubenzee and, in a clearly rehearsed speech, told waiting journalists, 'He is my friend. I have lots of men friends … I am often out with them.'

☞ *Walk back up the street and immediately turn right into Walton Street. After 300 metres, turn right into Lennox Gardens*

Mews. At the end, turn left into Milner Street, then immediately turn left again into Lennox Gardens. Number 38 is on the left.

Lennox Gardens

'Squidgygate tapes' James Gilbey.

Number 38 Lennox Gardens is the home of James Gilbey, often referred to as Diana's first real boyfriend. The pair dated briefly when Diana first moved to London in 1980. Diana was a shy, gawky teenager when they first met and Gilbey an affable, somewhat nerdy man about town.

They met again in the summer of 1989 at Julia Samuels's 30th birthday party. By that time, Diana's marriage was on the rocks and Gilbey, having also recently suffered in love, was just what she needed.

Gilbey, a charming and popular man who worked as a dealer in expensive cars, is the son of a family who had founded their fortunes on Gilbey's Gin and the nephew of the late distinguished Catholic cleric Monsignor Alfred Gilbey.

Throughout that summer of 1989, Diana and Gilbey resumed their friendship, and Diana often called at Gilbey's flat in Lennox Gardens. It was a private oasis. Anyone spotting Diana's car in the area always assumed she was at nearby Harrods or Harvey Nichols. They spent nearly the whole summer together and shared a weekend at a rented farm in Norfolk. Gilbey remains one of the most famous people in her life, although it has never been proven that they were anything more than good friends.

Gilbey's name was thrust into the public limelight when it was revealed he was the other man on the infamous 'Squidgygate tape' first published and broadcast by the *Sun* newspaper to an incredulous world in 1992. In the recording, obtained from their mobile-phone signals, Gilbey referred to Diana as 'Squidgy' and 'Squidge'. Diana also revealed to Gilbey that she didn't want to become pregnant. After the public uproar, Diana ditched her mobile phone in exchange for a pager (sometimes called 'Beeper') (see page 3 plate section).

In fact, it is widely believed that the secret services were responsible for the recording and leaking of the tape, and Diana herself was convinced that she was being bugged by MI5 when she discovered a device on the wheel arch of her BMW car (as revealed in the book *Diana and the Paparazzi* – Blake Publishing).

☞ *Continue past number 38 and turn left (the road remains Lennox Gardens). Walk 20 metres to the T-junction with Walton Street. Adjacent is Ovington Square.*

Diana's Secret Rendezvous

Richard Kay, the royal reporter for the *Daily Mail*, was Diana's favourite scribe. The pair had established a rapport early on in his stint as a royal reporter. Kay is charming, intelligent and a sympathetic listener, and they had enjoyed several off-the-record conversations at private receptions during foreign tours. Of course,

it helped that Kay's editor-in-chief
was none other than newspaper
doyen Sir David English, a man
who acted as Diana's unofficial
press adviser during the early years
of her marriage. In many ways,
Kay is the perfect royal reporter;
with his matinee-idol looks and
affable manner, he rarely looks out
of place among the titled gentry he
is writing about, seeming to belong
to a bygone age of chivalry and
respect. In uniform, he could be
a young subaltern, taking an
enlisted man's salute with ease, or a
naval commander at the deck of a
submerged submarine, binoculars
in hand, scanning the enemy coast.

As well as his good looks and
charm, Kay had two things going
for him that gave him a distinct
advantage over his Rat Pack
rivals. First, he worked for the
Daily Mail and, like all well-
heeled young ladies, Diana had
grown up with that paper, the
voice of middle England that

*Royal reporter Richard Kay
jumps into Diana's Audi parked
in Ovington Square.*

always harks back to a country that probably never existed.
Indeed, even in Neanderthal times, the *Daily Mail* would

probably have lamented nostalgically, 'Things haven't been the same since the dinosaurs left.'

Second, and more importantly, Kay is a *very* good reporter. His meteoric rise through the ranks from door-stepping hack to highly paid columnist is a tribute to his skill and dedication – a throwback to the days when reporters looked on their jobs as vocations rather than occupations; when the by-line was considered a bonus and hero-grams were Fleet Street's equivalent of being 'mentioned in dispatches'.

In early May 1994, Diana arranged a secret meeting with Kay, with the purpose of giving her side of the story following claims she had recently been photographed topless while sunbathing in Spain. At that time the protracted divorce proceedings between Diana and Prince Charles had just begun and the image of a

Diana walks towards her parked car in Ovington Square.

semi-naked Diana splashed across the foreign press was not desired. (To Diana's everlasting relief, the pictures were bought and buried by the owner of *Hello!* magazine, Eduardo Sanchez.)

Diana arranged to meet Kay in Ovington Square, and drove herself to the venue in her green Audi. She parked in the quiet Knightsbridge Street, a stone's throw from Harrods, to all intents just another Sloane Ranger out for a day's shopping. Very few people noticed Kay as he walked quickly up the street, opened the passenger door and slipped inside.

Unfortunately for the Princess, the hour-long car rendezvous and the conversation that took place turned out to be a public-relations disaster. A photographer captured the meeting, and the following day's *Sun* newspaper roared out the headline TWO-FACED DIANA, and the story went on to say, 'Princess Diana kept a secret rendezvous with top royal reporter – just hours after complaining about intrusions into her life.'

The impression given was that Diana was up to her old tricks again. Surely Diana couldn't exploit the press at the same time as she was condemning them?

And, unfortunately for both Diana and Kay, the next time they were photographed together was an even greater PR disaster and very nearly destroyed Diana's reputation forever (see page 4 plate section).

☞ *Cross over Walton Street and head right. The next road on your left is Beauchamp Place.*

Beauchamp Place

Beauchamp Place was Diana's favourite street in her favourite part of London. Situated in the heart of Knightsbridge,

Beauchamp Place, with its designer-label shops frequently attended by the world's most famous celebrities, is the Rodeo Drive of London.

Being a resident of the Royal Borough of Westminster and Chelsea, Diana had a parking permit that enabled her to beat the ever-prevailing parking problems of London. She always left her car in nearby Pont Street or Lennox Gardens, both south of Beauchamp Place.

As already mentioned, Diana's favourite restaurant was San Lorenzo, situated at number 22 Beauchamp Place, just a few shops away from the fashion emporium of Bruce Oldfield, always one of Diana's favourite designers. But, contrary to popular opinion, San Lorenzo was a royal favourite way before Diana first went there. Princess Margaret first discovered the small Italian eatery back in the days when it was known as an unpretentious bistro frequented by the in-crowd of the early Seventies. To this day, members of the paparazzi permanently lurk by its door and invariably manage to bag a celeb up the three steps that lead to the restaurant.

Diana arrives in Beauchamp place in her 'Wacko Jacko' outfit for an appointment at the Chinese acupuncturist.

When Diana first went to San Lorenzo, on Princess Margaret's advice, she immediately struck up a friendship with Mara Berni, San Lorenzo's popular owner. In Mara, Diana had a friend, an older woman with the life experience Diana was yet to have. Mara would often have a coffee alone with Diana, patiently listening to her many problems and offering earthy and sound advice.

Every friend Diana had was at some point taken to San Lorenzo, including James Hewitt and his three sisters. Princes William and Harry loved San Lorenzo and would often be taken on a Saturday with their mother after a trip to the Harbour Club. But San Lorenzo was not the only reason Diana was often seen in Beauchamp Place. Three times a week she used the services of a Chinese acupuncturist, where she was treated for the back pains that plagued her all her life. The surgery, once situated above a Portuguese restaurant, is no longer in practice (see page 5 plate section).

☞ *After viewing Beauchamp Place, return to Walton Street and turn left. Continue for 200 metres through Walton Place. Ahead of you is Harrods department store.*

Diana and Harrods

Mohammed Al Fayed is one of the most colourful figures in Britain today. The irascible tycoon, who rose from the slums of Egypt to become one of the richest men in the country, is rarely out of the newspapers. He gained control of elite store Harrods in 1985, having fought one of the bitterest business battles ever seen in London with his long-time rival Tiny Rowland. In a fit of pique, Rowland, owner of the *Sunday*

Mohammed Al Fayed and the Queen enjoy an afternoon at the Royal Windsor Horse Show.

Observer newspaper, rushed out a special mid-week edition, condemning Al Fayed's victory. But to the victor the spoils, and, on the top floor of Harrods, Al Fayed sat in his magnificent new office, chuckling as his assistant read out selected highlights of Rowland's vindictive words. Rowland called Al Fayed a 'gangster', Al Fayed called Rowland a ******. On balance it was felt that Al Fayed won by an expletive.

Successive British Home Secretaries, both Conservative and Labour, have refused to give Al Fayed a British passport, and his role in the cash-for-questions scandal that rocked Parliament in the early 1990s is thought to have brought down John Major's government.

But, for all that, most people see Mohammed Al Fayed as a lovable rogue, a cheeky chappy who had the nerve to take on the establishment.

Diana always had a soft spot for Al Fayed because of his relationship with her father, the 8th Earl Spencer. The contacts between the Spencer family and Al Fayed go back many years, and Al Fayed always claims he regarded Diana's father as a brother. It is widely acknowledged that Al Fayed had helped Johnny Spencer during the worst of his financial problems, and Johnny Spencer, in turn, helped Al Fayed with his naturalisation problems.

In fact, Diana was first introduced to the store by her father, who liked nothing better than discovering and buying the latest

Shopping for clothes in Harrods.

gadgets on sale. Sometimes Johnny Spencer could spend the whole day playing with the pocket calculators, digital watches and Sony Walkmans that, in those days, were only available to the very rich.

Diana was a regular customer at the famous store and often claimed it was the longest and most enduring relationship she ever had. Indeed, when she was a 16-year-old schoolgirl, Diana was asked where she would most like to live. 'In a penthouse above Harrods,' was her instant reply.

She visited the store at least once a week and Al Fayed told his staff to always inform him of her presence so that he could go down to greet her. Her stepmother, Raine, was a director of the company, and, at one point, Al Fayed invited the Princess to become a director but she refused on the grounds that it would not have been an appropriate position for her to take. Despite this, Diana continued to enjoy special status in the store, including an open account with unlimited purchasing powers, and she was allowed in to browse and buy at times when the store was closed to other customers. Latterly, she was also in the habit of popping into Al Fayed's office in the store to chat over a cup of coffee.

Diana arrives at Harrods for a morning of shopping in 1982.
Rex Features

But there were other contacts between Diana and Al Fayed quite separate from the pleasures and profits of shopping. Mohammed Al Fayed has been involved for many years in raising money for a wide variety of charities, so it was inevitable that they would often find themselves supporting the same cause and there were many meetings at charity balls, galas and dinners. It was after one of these meetings that Al Fayed raised the subject of Diana, William and Harry joining him, his wife Heini and their four children on a holiday to the French Riviera.

Such was Diana's relationship with Harrods, she was allowed her own private exit, a discreet tunnel that ran from the store under the Brompton Road and emerged into Trevor Square.

Today the tunnel is used for storage, as the exit was sealed up in 2002 after developers put up a block of luxury flats over it.

Just before Diana flew to Sardinia with Dodi Fayed on her last journey, she walked through the tunnel with Michael Cole, the Harrods spokesman who always accompanied her off the premises whenever she visited the store.

'She walked up the ramp, turned and waved to me,' says Michael. 'I can still see her now. She looked so beautiful, so happy and confident. She had so much to look forward to. "Goodbye, Michael," she called, then she was gone … and that was the last time I ever saw her.'

☞ *Cross the road and follow the building around to the right. Halfway down Basil Street, enter Harrods store. Just inside the doorway on the right is a bronze statue of Princess Diana and Dodi Fayed, named 'Innocent Victims'.*

☞ Go into the store and, at a statue of Mohammed Al Fayed, pass by to the left of it. Walk through the store to the far side of the cosmetics department and veer left. The Egyptian escalator is found through a doorway. On the lower ground floor is the candlelit shrine to Diana and Dodi.

Go back upstairs and exit Harrods by the doorway that leads to Hans Crescent. Turn left along the pedestrianised Hans Crescent to the end where it meets Brompton Road. Turn right along Brompton Road and continue for approximately 300

(Left) *The candle-lit shrine to Diana and Dodi and* (right) *the bronze statue named 'Innocent Victims'.*

metres. At the top of Sloane Street ahead of you is Harvey Nichols. Continue in the same direction along Knightsbridge with Harvey Nichols on your right until you reach Seville Street on your right-hand side. Walk into Seville Street. Fifty yards up on the right is the entrance to the Harvey Nichols fifth-floor restaurant.

Harvey Nichols

After Harrods, Harvey Nichols was Diana's favourite shop. It was the store where she bought all her personal girly gear. She loved *Vogue* magazine and used to read all their tips on make-up, often holding up a copy and telling friends it was her 'make-up bible'. Diana would often rip a page from the magazine, then go to Harvey Nichols to have a look. Diana liked nothing better than trying out new products, giggling like an excited schoolgirl as a sales assistant applied various lotions to the most famous face ever to grace the front cover of the very magazine she was holding. Diana never asked for special treatment at the store and never informed the management when she was coming in. She would drive to the store herself and park in a side street before secretly slipping in the rear entrance.

Diana loved the café on the fifth floor and, despite being the most famous person there, loved to go celebrity spotting. Diana would say to a friend, 'Look, there's so-and-so,' and then wave at them like a long-time friend, while the bemused celebrity tried to let everyone see who was waving at them. On one occasion Diana had lunch with Paul McCartney at the café and they both laughed as the in-house pianist played 'Yesterday' as they left the store. Paul McCartney tapped the pianist on the shoulder and said, 'That was lovely.' (See page 4 plate section).

☞ *Return to Knightsbridge and turn left, then left again into Sloane Street.*

Sloane Street remains one of the most glamorous parts of London. It is said that, if you stand for 15 minutes on Sloane Street, at some point a celebrity will walk by.

Virtually every designer name on earth can be seen on Sloane Street; outside the huge plate-glass doors ominous-looking doormen in dark suits and earpieces stand aside as the likes of Madonna, Angelina Jolie, Brad Pitt, Tom Cruise and Victoria

Casually shopping in Sloane Street. © Mark Saunders

Madonna buys a video in Sloane Street.

Beckham and their bodyguards alight from people carriers with tinted windows.

Madonna in particular names Sloane Street as her favourite part of London. When she lived in the city, she would sometimes dress down and, accompanied by a single bodyguard, cruise the street. Sometimes she would pop into the video store and, without any fanfare, look through the large selection of blockbusters available before making her choice and standing in the queue like any other punter.

Like so many other celebs, Diana's favourite shop was Gucci. She was often seen outside the upmarket store gazing in the window. Her stepmother Raine was also a fan of Gucci and often Diana and Raine would stroll down Sloane Street together after a lunch at nearby Harvey Nichols.

☞ *After approximately 900 metres, you will reach Sloane Square. In the far left corner is Sloane Square underground station.*

Sloane Square

Sloane Square is a small, hard-landscaped square on the boundaries of the fashionable London districts of Knightsbridge, Belgravia and Chelsea. The square is part of the unique Hans Town area designed in 1771 by Henry Holland Snr and Jnr. Both the town and the square were named after Sir Hans Sloane, whose heirs owned the land at the time.

The square lies at the east end of the trendy King's Road and is linked to Knightsbridge by Sloane Street. In the early 1980s, the area gave its name to the 'Sloane Rangers', the young, underemployed, often snooty and ostentatiously well-off members of the upper classes.

☞ *Take a District or Circle line train east for one stop to Victoria. Then take the Victoria line south for one stop to Pimlico. Alternatively, take a taxi from Sloane Square and ask the driver for the Young England Kindergarten at the north end of St Georges Square in Pimlico. Upon arrival at Pimlico tube station, walk eastwards along Bessborough Street for approximately 100 metres. St Georges Square can be found on the left. Walk down St Georges Square for 20 metres and just past a church on your right is the rear entrance to the Young England Kindergarten.*

Young England Kindergarten

Diana's last job before her marriage was at the Young England Kindergarten, in a church hall in St Georges Square, Pimlico, where she worked as an assistant and was known to the children as Miss Diana. The school, which then had ten teachers catering for about fifty children under the age of five, the offspring of well-heeled local residents, was run by Victoria Wilson and Kay Seth-Smith. Kay had been educated at Diana's school, West Heath, and so had her sister Janie, who had been there at the same time as Diana's sister Jane and it was through them that Diana was taken on to help.

Initially, Diana worked for three afternoons a week but later, when her natural affinity with children became obvious, she also began to work in the mornings.

Diana, who was once described by her mother as 'a positive Pied Piper with children', helped them with their artwork, tidied up, washed mugs and, when necessary, quelled arguments, dried tears and dispensed cuddles.

Once news of the royal romance broke in September 1980, Diana was besieged by journalists at the kindergarten. She wept when she saw photos of herself in the newspapers because, despite the excitement of her romance with Prince Charles, she knew she would have to leave the job.

After her engagement, Diana returned to the kindergarten, where the children climbed all over her and gave her a collage they had made as a memento. She invited all ten of her colleagues there to the royal wedding. Her youngest bridesmaid, five-year-old Clementine Hambro, Sir Winston Churchill's great-granddaughter, had been one of her favourite charges at Young England (see page 5 plate section).

☞ *Return to Bessborough Street. Turn left and, with the church on your left, continue for 20 metres along Lupus Street, then turn left into St Georges Square (west side). Twenty metres down on the left is the front entrance to the Young England Kindergarten. Return to Lupus Street and turn left. Walk 200 metres along Lupus Street until you meet traffic lights and turn right into St Georges Drive, then almost immediately right again into Denbigh Street. Number 71a can be found on the left-hand side of the street, about halfway down.*

Oliver Hoare heads for his Belgravia Club.

Pimlico

A matter of weeks before Diana made her time-and-space speech in October 1993, Oliver Hoare left his wife and moved into a smart apartment in Denbigh Street, Pimlico. Although Diana gave her reason for leaving public life as the pressure of her work, it was, in fact, Oliver Hoare's decision to leave his wife that prompted her to withdraw from any public role.

Diana was now close to her long-cherished dream that they may set up home together. And, although Pimlico wasn't exactly Italy, the dream location for Diana's new life, it was roughly in the right direction. She was head over heels in love with Hoare and he had demonstrated his commitment to the relationship by leaving his marital home.

Diana and Hoare spent many nights together in the basement flat but, ultimately, the affair was doomed. Diana's demands were simply too great for him; she wanted him to give up not just his family home, but his family as well. After five weeks in Pimlico, Hoare returned to his wife.

He never saw Diana again.

☞ *This is the end of Walk 2. The nearest tube station is Pimlico.*

WALK 3

THIS WALK INCLUDES:

Princess Diana – the mother / Secret Kensington Palace exits / Helicopters / Diana, Princess of Wales Memorial Playground / Diana, Princess of Wales Memorial Walk (section) / Secret rendezvous / Birthplace of the Princes / Hairdressers / Dentists / Clinics / Foot massage & colonic irrigation / Diana saves a life.

Length – *3.5 miles or 5.4 km*
Time – *4 hours*
Underground – *Notting Hill Gate*

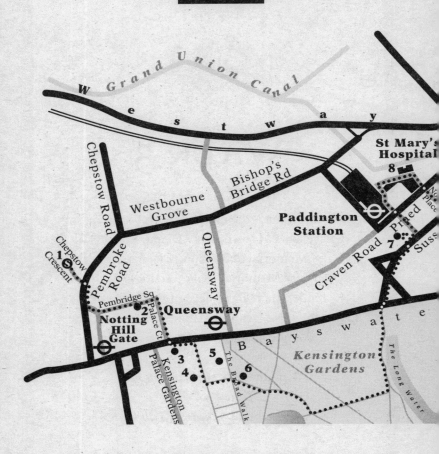

WALK 3

START **1.** Mrs Mynor's Nursery, 11 Chepstow Villas
2. Wetherby School
3. Black Gate
4. Helicopter Pad
5. Diana Princess of Wales Memeorial Playground
6. Diana Princess of Wales Memeorial Walk
7. Talbot Square 2nd rendezvous with Richard Kay
8. Lindo Wing, St Mary's Paddington

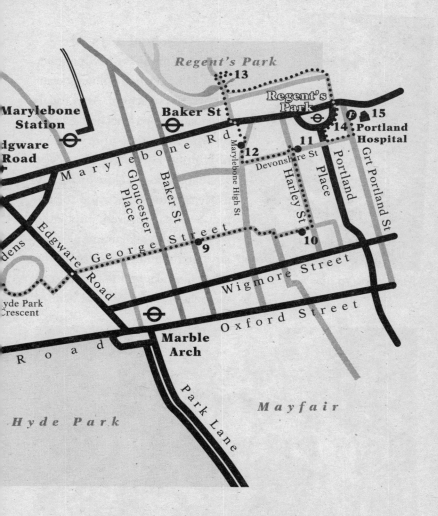

9. Daniel Galvin, Hairdresser
10. Dentist, 31 Queen Anne Street
11. Harley Street (Crescent Mews West)
12. Osteopath, 1 Oldbury Place
13. Regents Park
14. Harley Street Clinic
FINISH 15. Portland Hospital

School days

William emerges from his first day at nursery.

On a sunny day in September 1985, Prince William began his first day at school. After much discussion his parents had decided on Mrs Mynor's Nursery School in Notting Hill Gate. The venue was chosen for its close proximity to Kensington Palace and for the fact it wasn't entirely populated by the wealthy. Diana in particular loved the idle gossip with the other mothers and taking part in the 'school run', that great bane of

The world's press gather for the future King's arrival.

British commuters where middle-class mums drive their 2.6 children to school while chatting on their mobile phones, oblivious to all other vehicles.

Mrs Mynor's Nursery was a friendly, happy school with three classes of 12 pupils. On his first day, accompanied by his mother, William, wearing a bright-red pair of shorts and checked shirt, hardly blinked at the waiting photographers who assumed, incorrectly, he was merely nervous about his first day at school. William's main concern, however, had been an emotional scene at KP earlier that morning when Harry, just days after his first birthday, had let loose a torrent of tears when William had left.

The scene had upset Princess Diana as well, who had not realised how close Harry had become to his brother and how he could not bear to be parted from him.

Harry and William were separated two mornings each week and each time Harry would be reduced to tears. Eventually, his mother allowed Harry on the school run so he could spend precious more moments with his elder

Diana clutches the school itinerary as she leaves Mrs Mynor's.

brother. On one memorable occasion, Harry, accompanied by both his parents, saw William act in the school's nativity play. It was the first time he had been allowed to accompany his parents inside William's school. Later, back at KP, Harry insisted the whole event be immediately replayed with him taking on the role of the shepherd and Charles as an unlikely innkeeper.

In September 1987, Harry finally joined his brother at Mrs Mynor's. Unlike William, he had not been keen to start kindergarten and his first day at school was somewhat ruined by floods of tears that morning at KP. Harry clung to his mother throughout the ten-minute journey to the school from KP, during which she assured him she, too, had been terrified on her first day at school. Remembering her own miserable time at her finishing school in Switzerland, Diana almost gave in at one point and suggested to Harry's personal detective that maybe tomorrow would be a better day to start.

But, as soon as Harry saw the waiting throng of press photographers, a change seemed to come over him. He leaped from the car and proceeded to make funny faces towards the cameras, much to his mother's obvious joy and amusement. 'Harry, the Clown Prince', as the press immediately dubbed him, loved the audience and was quite prepared to play up to the cameras, something he still enjoys to this day.

There are three levels of schooling at Mrs Mynor's. The children started as Cygnets, moved up to Little Swans and eventually left the school as Big Swans. As well as a basic awareness of numbers and letters of the alphabet, the young charges were encouraged to paint and even make clay sculptures.

Harry, in particular, relished the painting sessions, when he could use crayons and paints with wild abandon, never noticing that most of the colour seemed to end up on him and not the white card.

The school also encouraged pupils to take part in the endless plays and concerts they put on for the parents. During the school's nativity play in 1988, Harry stole the limelight when he reprised his role as the shepherd which he had played at KP with his dad as innkeeper and Diana as Joseph. It was his first real taste of stardom and, as he stood on the stage at the end of the play, he relished the audience's applause, noting with pride how enthusiastically his own parents and brother William were clapping him (see page 4 plate section).

☞ *Facing the nursery, turn right back up to the crossroads. Turn left into Chepstow Crescent. At the end of Chepstow Crescent, walk across Pembridge Villas and head right. Take the second road on the left, Pembridge Square. With the centre of the square in front of you, ignore the left-hand road (Pembridge Square north) and walk to the right, then take the second left road (Pembridge Square south). Wetherby School can be found approximately halfway down Pembridge Square on the right-hand side at number 11.*

Wetherby School

The pre-kindergarten Wetherby School is located in Pembridge Square, just five minutes from KP at Notting Hill Gate. William's antics at the school are legendary, and still spoken about by his family today. Quite simply,

Prince Harry joins Prince William at Wetherby School watched by proud mother, Diana.

In his stride. William arrives for another day of school.

he was a little terror. When a small birthday party was thrown for another child at Wetherby, William ran riot, making loud noises and refusing to sit with the other children. Told to behave himself, he began to scream that he hated the food – sandwiches and ice cream – before picking up his plate and hurling it to the floor. Staff members instructed him to clean up the mess but William just stood there and declared, 'When I am King, I'm going to send all my knights around to kill you!'

'Pick it up,' one of the teachers ordered him.

William gritted his teeth and snarled, 'Do you know who I am?'

'Yes, you are a very naughty boy,' the teacher replied.

Soon teachers and children alike had a nickname for Prince William; they called him 'Basher'.

During one eventful sports day at the school, William pinched the bottom of a classmate's unsuspecting mother. Later, the heir to the throne decided to relieve himself on a bush next to the school. The next day, a tabloid ran two photographs of William caught in the act. The predictable head-line: The Royal Wee.

Diana's school run is over for the morning.

William, who was only six at the time, already had an eye for the ladies. Possibly following the example of one of his ancestors, Henry VIII, he proposed to five-year-old Eleanor Newton with the words: 'If you don't marry me, I'll put you in jail.' To another little girl, cast as the princess in a school play, he said matter-of-factly, 'You're too ugly. You have to look like my mum to be a princess.'

In June 1989, Diana showed up at Wetherby's sports day to run in the mothers' race, which she won. 'This is the first time in my life I've won anything like this,' she said excitedly.

But, when it was time to go home, William simply ignored his mum's calling and ran off to play with his friends. Diana, in turn, sprinted across the field, grabbed William by the arm and marched him to the car. In the process, paparazzi snapped Diana giving the boy a quick slap on the backside – a picture that inevitably ignited a firestorm of controversy.

☞ *Continue in the same direction and exit the square into Moscow Road. Take the second road, Palace Court, on your right. Walk to the end of the road. At the T-junction, find a suitable place to cross over the road to the south pavement of Bayswater Road. Walk eastwards (left) for approximately 15 metres. Just before a bus-stop shelter is the Black Gate.*

The Black Gate

Princess Diana's fight for a private life was a battle that was fought on three different fronts. She had to be wary of the Palace, the press *and* the public. Diana was easily the best-loved member of the Windsor household but, as she learned many times, the fickle public that loved her could easily turn against her. Diana's image was that of the beautiful, tortured princess, unloved by a callous husband who preferred the arms of his ageing mistress. It was an image Diana encouraged, which is one of the reasons she went to such lengths to protect it. As a senior member of the British Royal Family, there was a strong argument that she wasn't *entitled* to a private life but that argument was based on the assumption that senior royals didn't do anything the public would be remotely interested in. But Diana was the first ever soap-opera princess, and the press were far more interested in what went on behind palace doors than anything she did in public.

After Diana and Charles split in 1992, interest in Diana's life centred on only one thing: who would be the new man in her life? Diana had already had one major love affair the public was never aware of, with James Hewitt. But that was a romance condoned by Buckingham Palace. Diana had Hewitt, Charles had Camilla and, in public, they both still had each other.

Diana was forced to use subterfuge on a number of occasions to maintain her public image. In the dead of night, and without ceremony, a hand would appear through the centre hole in the Black Gate, carefully pulling through the chain without disturbing the quiet night calm. A solo policeman in uniform was the only collaborator in Diana's craftiness, for, as well as the press always on the lookout for unusual activities, there were also some of the Palace staff that on occasions would gossip about the activities of their charges enticed by the lure of the cheque books of Wapping.

The gates were pulled open briskly for the waiting Princess in her Audi. The policeman saluted, pleased with his night's work, and Diana sped out on to the road and disappeared into the traffic. From here, Diana was free to lead a normal life once she had escaped the confines of KP.

As well as secretly meeting her lovers, Diana would drive across London while talking on her hands-free mobile phone. This gave her the opportunity to speak freely without the worry of eavesdroppers at the Palace listening to her conversations and selling them to the press. But, unfortunately for Diana, even these phone calls didn't remain private, as we saw in the Squidgygate affair with James Gilbey. (See James Gilbey-Lennox Gardens in Walk 2.)

Discreet and alone, Diana drives along Gloucester Road.

☞ *Continue past an NCP car and coach park on your right, then enter Kensington Gardens by Orme Square Gate. Head down Jubilee Walk for approximately 20 metres. On the right, in the field, is the helicopter landing point.*

Helicopter at the ready

The Royal Family frequently use helicopters. The Queen has seven at her disposal in the royal fleet and, wherever the monarch is in residence, a helicopter is always on hand; contrary to popular opinion, the nearby helicopter is not kept for medical emergencies, but in case a royal evacuation is deemed necessary.

Prince Charles, who holds a helicopter pilot's licence, often travelled by helicopter to and from Highgrove. On one famous occasion, he was clambering into a royal chopper in a newly

Wessex helicopter of the Queen's Flight drops Diana off.

A smile and a wave, Diana departs for a visit in Wales.

pressed and cleaned suit when a two-year-old Prince William ambushed him with a mud pie. To his annoyance, Charles was informed by his personal detective he had mud all down his back and that it would probably be a good idea to change his suit.

Use of the helicopter pad at KP wasn't so easy, or so frequent. Because of the stringent control of London's skies, a helicopter could only be used in the most exceptional of circumstances.

It was, therefore, something of a controversy when a helicopter belonging to Harrods landed on the helipad at KP on 12 August 1997. Princess Diana had an appointment with a clairvoyant, Rita Rogers, in Derbyshire and had asked Dodi Fayed to come with her. Dodi, spotting an opportunity to impress Diana, asked his father if he could use the official Harrods chopper. Consent was given and Diana and Dodi flew to Chesterfield that afternoon.

When word of the visit to the fortune-teller reached Fleet

Street, news photographers raced to KP to capture their arrival back in London. Dodi was incensed: 'How did they find out?' he demanded of Michael Cole, Harrods' official spokesperson.

But the Queen was even angrier, and demanded to know why a helicopter had been given permission to land at a royal residence 'simply to take Diana to see a witch doctor'.

The message to Diana was clear: there were to be no more helicopter trips from Kensington Palace.

☞ *With your back to the helicopter landing field, walk across to the Diana, Princess of Wales Memorial Playground.*

Diana, Princess of Wales Memorial Playground

A huge wooden pirate ship is the amazing centrepiece of the Diana, Princess of Wales Memorial Playground. This children's wonderland opened on the 30 June 2000 in memory of the late Princess.

Located next to her Kensington Palace home, the playground is a fitting tribute to the Princess who loved the innocence of childhood and everything connected with children.

Over 750,000 children enjoy this free playground each year. Kids love to play, explore, dash about and let their imaginations run riot in this magical space. There is a sensory trail, a beach around the pirate ship and various toys and play sculptures, all set against a lush backdrop of trees and plants.

And there is plenty of seating so the grown-ups can relax too.

The designers have created an extensive area where less able and able-bodied children can play together, and which seeks to provide for the physical, creative, social and educational development of all children. Inspired by the stories of Peter Pan, the playground encourages children to explore and follow their imaginations, always learning while they play. Next to the playground is a statue of Peter Pan created by J Willhouse in 1932. Interestingly, it was used as a 'drop-box' by the nearby Russian Embassy during the Cold War.

☞ *Pick up the Diana, Princess of Wales Memorial Walk on The Broad Walk just south of the playground. A plaque in the ground marks the starting point. Take the arrowed route in the eastward direction, not the route along The Broad Walk.*

Follow this marked route for 900 metres until you reach The Fountains on your right. Stay in the same direction and leave the park by the Marlborough Gates ahead of you. Cross the Bayswater Road and walk up the right-hand side of Lancaster Terrace. At the top, walk over the crossing, then over another on Westbourne Street. On the east side of Westbourne Street, continue up Sussex Gardens for 50 metres. Talbot Square can be found on the left side of the street.

Secret rendezvous in Talbot Square

The genius of Diana's plan was in its simplicity. The paparazzi had been informed of all movements that afternoon. Diana had arranged to meet Richard Kay in leafy Talbot Square in West London. Diana drove up in her Audi, at that time one of the most easily recognisable vehicles in the world. Diana had been featured in the newspapers driving the Audi dozens of times; on one occasion she had driven William and Harry to the Harbour Club with the convertible roof down, hardly the subtlest attempt to appear incognito. Wearing a baseball cap pulled well down over her face (a disguise about as effective as trying to hide the Statue of Liberty by covering the torch with a blanket), casual jacket and jeans, Diana parked the car opposite Kay's Volvo.

Less than 50 yards behind her, the paparazzi also parked their vehicles and gleefully picked up their 500mm lenses.

Kay, dressed in jeans and open-necked shirt, as if he had been summoned hastily, waved at Diana. He immediately got out of his car, ran over and jumped into Diana's Audi, every moment captured by the

Another secret rendezvous with Richard Kay. Diana was desperate to avoid another scandal. Top and bottom © Glenn Harvey/Antony Jones.

lenses of the paparazzi, who, immediately recognising the *Daily Mail* reporter, couldn't believe their luck.

For 20 minutes, Diana and Kay sat in her car talking. They stopped when a member of the public rapped on the car window and told them they were being photographed from across the road. That was exactly what Diana wanted. They then both got out of her car and moved across the road to his Volvo and drove off. Three hours later, they returned, Kay took Diana to her car and waved goodbye.

During the three hours they were away, Kay had phoned the *News of the World* from a public call box to explain he was speaking on behalf of the Princess of Wales to tell the newspaper there had been a mix-up, that Diana could not possibly have made the malicious phone calls at the times stated because she had been somewhere else.

Diana knew this wouldn't make any difference. The *News of the World* had a hell of a story and a few kind words from Richard Kay were not going to spoil it. Inevitably, the following day's paper screamed out the headline DI'S CRANKY PHONE CALLS TO MARRIED TYCOON, and, unsurprisingly, by noon, the story was making headlines all over the world.

That Sunday morning, newsmen and photographers besieged Diana as she went to play tennis at the Harbour Club as usual. Wearing her favourite American-style sweatshirt, ultra-short light-blue shorts and trainers, she smiled happily for the cameras, appearing not to have a care in the world. The waiting newsmen threw questions at her but she said nothing; all that she wanted to say had been said to Mr Kay the previous day.

Back at the newsroom of the *Daily Mail*, it was decided that it would look ridiculous to claim Richard Kay's by now world-exclusive story had come from a 'close pal' in light of the paparazzi pictures that had already been sold to the *Sun*. The decision was taken to admit they were running Diana's words, which was always what Diana had wanted.

For the first time in history, a senior member of the Royal Family had gone 'on the record' to deny a story in a tabloid newspaper.

☞ *Continue in the same direction up Sussex Gardens and take the first left turning into London Street. Walk to the T-junction and cross over the main road (Praed Street), then continue further along London Street. Take the third right into South Wharf Road. The Lindo Wing is about 25 metres on the right along South Wharf Road.*

St Mary's, Paddington

Prince William was born in a 12ft x 12ft, £200-a-day room in the Lindo Wing of St Mary's Hospital, just a stone's throw from London's Paddington train station.

There were no surprises as far as the sex of the baby was concerned. Although Charles and Diana repeatedly told the press they had no idea if their firstborn was to be male or female, they knew what to expect from sonograms taken in the third trimester. Regardless of the baby's gender, Diana was also determined to do something else that was anathema to most royal mothers – breastfeed the child.

William did not come easily; the labour tuned out to be as difficult as the pregnancy. At one point, Diana's temperature soared so high that her doctors considered an emergency Caesarean. But after 16 gruelling hours and with relief from an epidural, Diana at last gave birth to a blue-eyed, 7lb 1.5oz baby boy at 9.03pm on 21 June 1982.

Charles was at his wife's side throughout the delivery. At the moment his son appeared, Charles whispered to Diana, 'Fantastic, beautiful. You are a darling.' By contrast, his own father, Prince Philip, had been playing squash with an equerry while Charles was being born.

A crudely lettered cardboard sign was posted on the hospital gates: IT'S A BOY. Church bells across Paddington rang, in Hyde Park cannons boomed, and throughout the length and breadth of the United Kingdom toasts were made welcoming the future King.

Charles was uncharacteristically emotional emerging from the hospital two hours later with lipstick on his cheek, and he shook the hands of jubilant well-wishers.

'Nice one, Charlie!' shouted one loyal subject. 'Give us another.'

'Bloody hell,' Charles replied. 'Give us a chance.'

The next day, Her Majesty the Queen, clutching her ever-present handbag, visited the hospital. 'Thank goodness, he doesn't have ears like his father's,' the Queen said, laughing.

Only 21 hours after the difficult birth, Diana walked out of the hospital with a beaming Charles, who cradled William in a lace shawl. To the cheers of the waiting throng, they posed for the photographers, then got into the waiting royal car and sped off to their new home, Kensington Palace.

Just over two years later, Diana was back at the hospital for the birth of her second child, Harry. Because of the awful morning sickness Diana had suffered during her pregnancy with

William, the Queen had ordered Diana to take things easier this time round. Diana had been brought to Windsor Castle, the Queen's favourite home, in the final weeks of her pregnancy, as the Queen had considered the peace and tranquillity of her favourite home to be the perfect place for the exhausted Princess to get some much needed rest.

Diana's labour pains began early on Saturday morning, 15 September 1984. She was immediately taken back to St Mary's Hospital, where she arrived with her husband at 7.30am.

Once again a room had already been prepared for Diana in the hospital's Lindo Wing and it was here she was taken, with Prince Charles in attendance, to be examined by her gynaecologist, Dr George Pinker, the man who had taken care of William's birth two years earlier.

Harry was born at 4.20pm that afternoon, some three hours after Diana's contractions had begun to increase in number. It was not a perfect birth and, at one point, Diana was again given the painkilling epidermal injection she had received during William's birth.

Throughout the ordeal Diana sucked on an ice cube, with Prince Charles by her side, constantly mopping her brow and endlessly repeating words of encouragement.

Harry weighed in at 6lb 14oz, and had light-blue eyes and a bit of reddish hair. Diana had again known her second child would be a boy as it had been revealed during an ultra-scan.

Prior to leaving St Mary's, Diana thanked all the staff personally. She then had her hair and make-up done in preparation for the fifty or so photographers who were waiting outside, along with an astonishing 1,500 jubilant onlookers.

Prince Charles and Princess Diana present their newborn, Prince Harry, on the top step of the Lindo wing entrance.

Looking fresh and stunning in a smart red suit with a red-and-white striped blouse, fashionably tied at the neckline, and cradling Harry in her arms, Diana greeted her public. Unfortunately for the waiting crowds, Harry was covered in a white shawl and both press and public were disappointed to catch only a glimpse of hair and the tip of a nose.

Charles more than made up for the somewhat disappointing photo op by supplying the Rat Pack with some excellent copy. He told a friendly press corps his son was 'absolutely marvellous' and added, 'We have nearly got a full polo team now.'

☞ *The walk continues to the next point, Daniel Galvin at 58–60 George Street, London WIU 7ET, at just over one mile. If preferred, take a taxi or travel by underground to Marble Arch.*

From the Lindo Wing, retrace your steps along South Wharf Road, then London Street until you arrive at Praed Street. At the junction of London Street and Praed Street, the stairs to Paddington tube station are on your right. Take the Circle or District line southbound for two stops and change trains at Notting Hill Gate. Take the Central line eastbound for three stops and get off at Marble Arch.

As you exit Marble Arch station, turn right and walk to the junction of Great Cumberland Place on your right. Walk up Great Cumberland Place for 350 metres to the third intersection, and turn right into George Street. At approximately 300 metres on the left of George Street is Daniel Galvin Hairdressers at numbers 58–60.

☞ *Walking directions continued from the Lindo Wing*
Keeping on the right-hand side of the road, keep going further up

the road and take the next right. Ahead of you is an archway over the road. Walk under the arch and cross back over Praed Street into the adjacent Norfolk Place. At the end of Norfolk Place, cross over Sussex Gardens into the adjacent Radnor Place. Take the first left into Somers Crescent. At the end, turn left into Hyde Park Crescent and follow the left-curved road until on the left is Oxford Square. Walk up Oxford Square, then turn right into Porchester Place. After 100 metres, take the next left into Kendal Street. Walk eastwards along Kendal Street and cross over the busy Edgware Road, then into the adjacent George Street. After 650 metres, Daniel Galvin, at numbers 58–60, can be found on the left.

Daniel Galvin

In today's messed-up world of instant fame, the word 'celebrity' has little value. There is no facet of life that doesn't have a celebrity aspect. Our TVs and newspapers are full of celebrity chefs, celebrity designers, celebrity lawyers, celebrity make-up artists, celebrity mums, celebrity wives, celebrity girlfriends and, in the case of Paris Hilton, we even have a celebrity celebrity.

Hairdresser Daniel Galvin, however, is the exception, for he genuinely is one of the world's most sought-after hairdressers and, when it comes to mixing with the rich and famous, he's seen it, done it and probably styled the T-shirt.

Apart from Princess Diana, Galvin's clients have included Madonna, Tom Cruise, Richard Gere, Nicole Kidman, Catherine Zeta Jones and Mel Gibson. He has also been the hair stylist for a number of major Hollywood productions, including the Oscar-winning *Braveheart*.

Diana experimented with many hairstyles. This hairstyle was fashioned for a visit to Ealing, London.

Galvin made his name in the early Seventies when, due to his unique ability to highlight hair and make it appear completely natural, he became known as the 'King of Colour'. Today he is considered to be one of the world's leading hair colourists.

Diana first met Galvin in the early 1980s. For some time she had been having her hair lightened, as her natural colour was mousey and, after this fact was reported in the newspapers, it set off a massive fashion trend for 'Di Lights', as Fleet Street predictably called them.

Daniel Galvin reported that highlighting at his West End salon had gone up 100% since Diana had come on the scene.

In July 1990, Diana was looking for a 'new look' to go with her more mature approach to her work. She was nearly 30 by now and anxious to lose the 'shy-Di' tag that she loathed.

Leaving Daniel Galvin's with another new hairstyle.

In the summer of that year, Diana emerged from Daniel Galvin's salon with her hair restyled. Scottish crimper Sam McKnight had given her the unique short elfin cut that was immediately copied around the world.

Diana loved going to the salon in George Street. Despite the fact any number of top hairdressers would have raced to KP for a private styling at the drop of a hat, Diana preferred the idle gossip and chitchat of the busy salon (see page 6 plate section).

☞ *Continue further along George Street until you arrive in Thayer Street. Walk across and head into the street adjacent, Marylebone Lane. Take the third left turning, Bulstrode Street. At the end, turn right into Wellbeck Street, then left into Queen Anne Street. The dentist is at number 31 on the right-hand side of the street.*

At the dentist

William is in no rush to get into the dentist chair.

It was inevitable, given William's love for contact sports, that he would suffer various injuries from time to time. Princess Diana fretted endlessly about this. She knew that William always had to be in the thick of the action. On the soccer field he was the captain, always shouting for the ball, a skilful footballer with a unique ability to 'bend it like Beckham'.

But it was playing rugby that caused William his most serious sporting injury. The incident happened at Eton College during the spring term of 1995, when William clashed head on with a much larger and stronger boy, and was momentarily unconscious. He was taken from the field to the school matron, who diagnosed a very mild form of concussion. Following consultation with Diana at KP, it was decided not to take William to hospital to get looked over, and, instead, a local doctor recommended by the school was dispatched to give William a thorough check-up. At the same time, his mother drove herself to the school. William was fine but, as well as

Emerging after treatment.

a knock to the head, he also lost a tooth in the incident. The following day, the school granted William permission to travel to London with his mother, where they visited a dentist in Queen Anne Street. William had a temporary replacement tooth put in. Afterwards, his mother asked if he would like to stay at KP that night. William, anxious to get back to his friends, declined the offer and was driven straight back to Eton after saying goodbye to his mother on the pavement (see page 6 plate section).

☞ *Continue further along Queen Anne Street and turn left into Harley Street. Walk 350 metres up Harley Street. Park Crescent Mews West is on your right just after a red post box.*

Retrace your steps along Harley Street to the first crossroads at Devonshire Street. Turn right and after 200 metres turn right at the T-junction. Walk north on Marylebone High Street, then

Diana frequently parked her Audi in Park Crescent Mews West for a doctor's appointment in Harley Street (see page 6 of the plate section).

take the second left, which is a small passageway hidden between shop fronts, called Olbury Place. Number 1 is straight ahead of you and slightly left.

Michael Skipwith

Diana loved alternative therapists, and, suffering from possibly stress-related back pain, she began seeing world-famous osteopath Michael Skipwith, who used rhythmic stretching and pressure to relieve tension in her back for the relatively low fee of £35 a session.

The sessions were so successful that Skipwith also began treating Diana for the headaches that periodically reduced her to tears, such were their severity. Diana had always believed she suffered from migraines but, following an initial check-up, Skipwith assured her they were not migraines, but headaches brought on by stress, the same cause of the problem she was having with her back.

Skipwith's healing hands cured Diana of her headaches as well as the back pains, although he did discover the great bane in the life of any doctor that treated Diana; he was expected to be on call 24 hours a day. Sometimes Diana would phone him in a near panic, asking for an immediate appointment. Diana always maintained her headaches and back

The treatment with Michael Skipwith worked wonders for Diana.

pain disappeared within 30 minutes of her latest appointment.

In early 1996, Diana took delivery of a state-of-the-art BMW-5 series, valued at £40,000 but at no cost to her. The makers were more than compensated by a royal endorsement during an impromptu press conference on the pavement outside Skipwith's Marylebone clinic. 'Isn't it lovely?' she told the waiting photographers. 'I'm only borrowing it but it's great.'

☞ *Return to Marylebone High Street through the passageway and turn left. Continue for 40 metres, then turn left through iron gates into the grounds of St Marylebone Parish Church. Head right, past the church, then walk across the main church entranceway. Take the pedestrian crossing over Marylebone Road into York Gate. You are now entering Regent's Park. At*

The beautiful setting of Regent's Park.

the traffic lights at the Outer Circle, continue in the same direction to York Bridge. Just after the bridge on the right is a footpath to a nature area.

Diana, lifesaver

In early May 1994, Diana had left KP and was heading for her stepmother's house in Belgravia. For once, she had decided not to drive herself and had procured the use of one of the royal chauffeurs to take her the short distance.

As the car drove through Regent's Park, Diana and the driver were forced to stop by a young girl who had run into the road, frantically waving her arms and pointing to the bridge over a small tribute that runs to the Serpentine.

Diana leaped from the vehicle and asked what on earth was wrong. The distressed girl, a young Finnish student, told her a man had fallen into the river.

Diana, the student and her chauffeur raced down the bank. At the

Diana looking very pleased with herself.

edge they could see a man floating in the water and they later learned he was called Martin O'Donoghue. With the help of the Finnish student, Diana's chauffeur pulled him out of the water as the Princess, who was holding their mobile phones and wallets, watched anxiously. Fortunately help had come in time and by the time the ambulance arrived Martin, whose nickname was Paddy, was sitting on the riverbank with Diana, talking. She followed the ambulance to the hospital, and, after Mr O'Donoghue had been admitted, Diana left her personal details with the hospital staff. She then went back into the room where Mr O'Donoghue had been taken and squeezed his hand. 'God bless you, Paddy,' she said tenderly.

Martin O'Donoghue (who has since changed his name by deed poll) never forgot what the Princess did for him. For the next three years, he met Diana at least once a week. Whenever she had a birthday or anniversary, he made a point of giving her some flowers or a present. The week before she died, he had delivered 100 red roses to her door to mark the first anniversary of her divorce. Diana, who had given the guards on the gates orders he was to be let through, came out and received them personally. She shook his hand and smiled. 'Thank you, Paddy,' she said. Then she turned and went back into KP. 'And that was the last time I ever saw her,' Mr O'Donoghue said.

Today he still leaves flowers on the anniversary of Diana's death, standing alone in tribute to the woman that saved his life. 'If it wasn't for her, I wouldn't be here today,' he says sadly.

☞ *Returning back to York Bridge from the nature area, turn left just after you cross over and walk into the park. Keep to the right-hand path, which runs parallel with the road (Outer*

Circle). After 500 metres, exit the park at the furthest south-eastern corner. Cross over the Outer Circle into Park Square East. At the traffic lights at the end, take the pedestrian crossing over Marylebone Road. Turn left and you can see a curved Regency-styled terrace building on your right in Park Crescent. The Hale Clinic is at number 7.

Hale Clinic

Diana was a great lover of alternative medicine, and was inclined to believe whatever her latest medical guru told her. This included the benefits of the process of colonic irrigation.

Three times a week, Diana would go to London's prestigious Hale Clinic for this practice, thought to have been started by the ancient Egyptians, which involved a super-enema that washes the bowels out with up to 12 gallons of water.

Diana swore by the process, claiming it pumped up her energy and kept her looking young. She even credited the enema treatment with curing her of fatigue, allergies, depression, infections, migraines and the bulimia that had haunted her throughout her marriage.

Each time she visited the Hale Clinic, Diana would be placed on

Diana leaving the Hale Clinic.

Prince Harry and Princess Diana leave the Portland hospital after visiting his newborn cousin, Princess Beatrice.

a couch and modestly covered. Distilled water was then pumped into her colon through a tube connected to a large stainless-steel pump apparatus. The water is body temperature and washes out years of collected faecal matter, mucous and built-up poisons. The whole process, for which Diana paid £50 a visit, was over in 40 minutes and was capped off with a special brew of acidophilus tea, which restores good bacteria to the system.

Although Diana was convinced the treatment was a miraculous cure-all, Prince Charles was horrified by her quirky health kick, telling her he found the whole process 'disgusting and distasteful' (see page 6 plate section).

☞ *Walk past the clinic keeping it on your left-hand side and continue around the curved pavement. At the end of the block, turn left into Portland Place, then next left into Devonshire Street. At the T-junction, turn left into Great Portland Street and the Portland Hospital is found on the left-hand side of the street.*

Portland Hospital

The Portland Hospital is notable for being used by the rich and famous of London. The private hospital is dedicated to the care of women and children exclusively. One of its royal patients has included the Duchess of York, who gave birth to Princess Beatrice and Princess Eugenie there in 1988 and 1990, respectively. Lady Helen Taylor, Claudia Schiffer, Victoria Beckham, Geri Halliwell, Gillian Anderson and Melanie Brown, among others, have all given birth to their children here.

Princess Diana, a good friend at the time of Sarah Ferguson, Duchess of York, was a regular visitor, bringing Prince William

and Prince Harry to see their new cousins, Beatrice and Eugenie. On one visit Prince William berated Prince Harry after spotting him poking his tongue out at the waiting newsmen, shouting, 'Stop it, Harry. That's very naughty.'

Sarah Ferguson and Prince Andrew present Princess Beatrice outside the Portland hospital.

☞ *To find your way to the nearest tube station – Great Portland Street – continue walking up Great Portland Street until you see it at the end of the road on the right.*

Walk 3 visitor information

En-route refreshments in Kensington Gardens
Diana, Princess of Wales Memorial Playground – Café
Queen Anne's Alcove – Café (near Marlborough Gate)

En-route refreshments in Regent's Park
Pavilion at the Tennis Centre –
Café (near to York Bridge and Nature area)
Avenue Gardens – Café (summer only)

En-route public toilets
Kensington Gardens: Inverness Terrace Gate / Marlborough Gate
Regent's Park: Between Avenue Gardens and Outer Circle

WALK 4

Length – *2 miles or 3.2 km*
Time – *1½ hours*
Underground – *Hyde Park Corner*
Bus routes – *2, 10, 15, 36, 73, 74, 82, 137, 148,*
414 and 436 go to Park Lane.
Request 'London Hilton'.

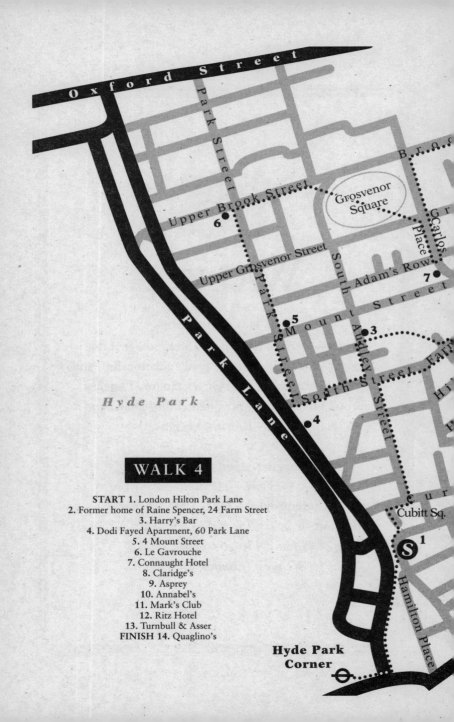

Oxford Street

Park Street

Upper Brook Street

6

Grosvenor Square

Bro

Gr Carlos Place

Gr

Upper Grosvenor Street

South Audley Street

Adam's Row

7

Park Street

Mount Street

5

3

South Audley Street

South Street

Fair

Hi

Hyde Park

Park Lane

4

Cubitt Sq.

S **1**

Hamilton Place

WALK 4

START 1. London Hilton Park Lane
2. Former home of Raine Spencer, 24 Farm Street
3. Harry's Bar
4. Dodi Fayed Apartment, 60 Park Lane
5. 4 Mount Street
6. Le Gavrouche
7. Connaught Hotel
8. Claridge's
9. Asprey
10. Annabel's
11. Mark's Club
12. Ritz Hotel
13. Turnbull & Asser
FINISH 14. Quaglino's

Hyde Park Corner

☞ *Exit Hyde Park Corner station to Park Lane east. Walk up Park Lane and after 100 metres the London Hilton is on your right at 22 Park Lane, London W1K 1BE.*

London Hilton

Almost a year had passed since the official separation of the Prince and Princess of Wales, and, on Friday, 3 December 1993, Diana was due to be guest of honour at a charity luncheon at the Hilton Hotel in aid of Headway National Head Injuries Association. The best-selling author Jeffery Archer had been summoned to the Palace to prepare Diana for the speech she was due to give. Archer had no idea at that time it was to be one of the most emotional and explosive speeches Diana ever made.

Archer realised it was going to be dramatic when Diana greeted him with the words, 'I'm not going to cry ... whatever happens, I'm not going to cry.'

At the Hilton the following day, the atmosphere was electric, the media expectant and the Princess visibly nervous, her hands shaking throughout the simple meal of avocado salad, tomato and

Diana announces her retirement from public life at the London Hilton hotel.

mozzarella cheese. The Princess kept her eye on Archer, the Master of Ceremonies, to make sure all was running to plan.

At the appropriate moment, she walked to the podium. Then, in a sometimes quavering, yet defiant voice, she appealed for 'time and space' after more than a decade in the spotlight. During her five-minute speech, she spoke of the unrelenting media exposure and, while she singled out the Queen and Duke of Edinburgh for their 'kindness and support', Diana never once mentioned her estranged husband.

In a voice choking with tears, Diana said, 'When I started my public life twelve years ago, I understood that the media might be interested in what I did. I realised then that their attention would inevitably focus on both our private and public lives. But I was not aware of how overwhelming that attention would become; nor to the extent to which it would affect both my public duties and my personal life, in a manner that has been hard to bear.'

While indicating that she would continue to support a small number of charities while she set about rebuilding her private life, Diana emphasised, 'My first priority will be to our children, William and Harry, who deserve as much love, care and attention as I am able to give, as well as an appreciation of the tradition into which they were born.'

After a 45-second thank-you speech by Jeffery Archer, the Princess left the Hilton's Grand Ballroom to an emotional standing ovation.

Her new life had begun.

☞ *Facing the London Hilton main entrance, walk down the left-hand side of the building, then left into Curzon Place. At Curzon*

Street, turn right then take the next left into South Audley Street. Walk north for approximately 150 metres, then turn right into South Street. After about 100 metres, when the road bends left at the Punchbowl pub (owned by Guy Ritchie), the road name changes to Farm Street. Raine Spencer's former house is at number 24 on the right.

Raine Spencer

Following her emotional speech at the Hilton, Diana decided her new life could only be complete if she cleared out the skeletons in her cupboard. Her refreshing openness and willingness to build bridges was both a sign of her growing maturity and determination to lay the ghosts of her past to rest as she tried to build a new life. This newfound resolve was at the heart of her emotional reconciliation with her stepmother Raine

Raine, the Countess Spencer and Count Jean-François Pineton de Chambrun on their wedding day.

Spencer. It was no secret that Diana, her sisters and brother had little love for the woman they called 'Acid Raine'. Stories that the furious Princess once pushed her down the stairs, had a screaming match with her at her brother's wedding and giggled at sneering accounts of her subsequent marriage to French aristocrat Count Jean-François de Chambrun were part of Spencer folklore – and made lurid newspaper headlines.

When her father, Earl Spencer, died, Diana could have been excused for consigning Raine to the dustbin of her life but she chose not to do so, inviting Raine and her French husband to lunch. It was an emotional encounter. The talk was of the past, reminiscing about the life of the late Earl Spencer. When the Princess thanked Raine for loving her father, in sickness and in health, Raine's famous composure cracked and she burst into tears. That meeting was a turning point in their relationship. Afterwards, Diana would often be seen at Raine's Belgravia house (situated opposite the Punchbowl pub) or dining at Claridges Hotel just a few streets away.

Former home of Raine, the Countess Spencer.

But not everybody was happy with this turn of events; the news that Diana and Raine were meeting frequently had a frosty reception from the rest of the Spencers. On one occasion, her mother, Frances Shand Kydd, angrily confronted Diana and demanded to know what the hell she thought she was doing. Diana explained patiently that, before her father died, he had asked her to watch over Raine. It was a promise she intended to keep. She pointed out that, as she hated Raine most and yet had been able to forgive and forget, so should the rest of the family (see page 7 plate section).

☞ *Retrace your steps for 20 metres and on the right-hand side of South Street you will find a small alleyway between two red-bricked buildings. There is a doorway at 49 South Street. Walk down the passageway into an open area of parkland called Mount Street Gardens. Walk diagonally across to the other side of the park and exit through the gates into South Audley Street. Harry's Bar is on the right-hand side.*

Turn south along South Audley Street and, after 50 metres, turn right into South Street. Walk to the end and, at the T-junction with Park Lane, turn left. Dodi Fayed's apartment is Number 60 Park Lane on your left.

Harry's Bar and Dodi's apartment

The most important week in Diana and Dodi's relationship began on Monday, 11 August 1997, when their friendship intensified and they spent every day of that week in each other's company. In total, Diana and Dodi only knew each other for six weeks and, of those six weeks, they spent just 25 days together.

On that Monday, Diana was at KP and Dodi was at his swish apartment at number 60 Park Lane. All that separated the couple was the green expanse of Hyde Park. During a telephone conversation, Dodi said to Diana, 'Why are we talking on the phone when you could be here?'

Diana immediately jumped into her car and drove the short distance to Park Lane.

The following day, Diana invited Dodi to come along to visit her clairvoyant near Chesterfield, in Derbyshire. It was an important gesture for Diana, since Rita Rogers, who had been recommended by the Duchess of York, had become a very important figure in Diana's life. The clairvoyant had already performed a reading on Dodi by satellite phone and told him it appeared he would never have another girlfriend.

On Wednesday, 13 August 1997, Diana and Dodi arranged a night on the town. She went to his apartment at 8.30pm and, after watching a private screening of *Air Force One*, starring Harrison Ford, they went back to number 60 Park Lane. Rather than pop out again for food, Dodi rang nearby Harry's Bar and had a takeaway delivered. They then sat on the floor together

and ate as George Michael played softly on the stereo. Diana eventually left at 2am. The next evening it was the same routine. Diana got to Dodi's at 7.45pm. This time they did not leave the Park Lane apartment, preferring to order a takeaway yet again from Harry's Bar, and Diana did not get back to KP until the small hours.

On the Friday of that week, the pair were briefly separated when Diana left London for a

Harry's Bar.

Eating out.

long-planned vacation in Greece with Rosa Monckton, during which time Diana began to have doubts about her relationship with Dodi. She was aware that newspaper reports in London were openly criticising her friendship with a man most people dismissed as an 'Arab playboy'. In Fleet Street's eyes, the only thing Dodi Fayed had ever shown an aptitude for was spending his father's money. He went through fast cars and celebrity girl-friends at an alarming rate, and enjoyed a decadent playboy lifestyle. Indeed, it seemed that Dodi's somewhat erratic lifestyle had begun to catch up with him. Dodi had sealed his love for his latest girlfriend, the model Kelly Fisher, with a cheque for £200,000. Unfortunately for the Californian beauty, it bounced. It appeared that, during his romance with Diana, Dodi had also forgotten he was engaged to Kelly Fisher. On the eve of Diana's departure for Greece, Kelly and her attorney, Gloria Allred, held a press conference in LA to announce she was suing Dodi for breach of contract. And, as Diana sailed around the Greek Isles, Dodi left Heathrow for LA to try to pacify his furious and by now extremely ex-fiancé, and sort out his complicated Californian finances.

Just 36 hours after arriving in LA, Dodi rushed back to London so he could be there when Diana returned from Greece. Diana arrived back at noon and by 9.00pm that night she was back at number 60 Park Lane for yet another takeaway from Harry's Bar. This time she is reported to have stayed until 1.15am. The next evening, at 6.40pm, they took off for a final Mediterranean cruise.

Whether Diana and Dodi were ever lovers remains open to doubt. The evidence we have (the *genuine* evidence, not the endless speculation) errs on the side of a close friendship rather than a sexual relationship. It is true they enjoyed each other's company and spent as much time together as they could but Diana did not show as much enthusiasm for the relationship as she had in previous times. When Diana was in love she screamed it from the rooftops. Whether it was Prince Charles, James Hewitt, Oliver Hoare or Hasnat Khan, every one of Diana's close friends *knew* she had fallen again. But with Dodi Fayed, Diana's feet seemed to be firmly on the ground.

After the original holiday in the South of France, where their relationship is said to have begun, Diana arrived back at KP to find four dozen roses and a £6,000 gold watch waiting for her – gifts from Dodi. Rather than squealing with delight, as she did when Oliver Hoare sent gifts of Islamic art, Diana seemed embarrassed, describing them as 'a bit over the top', although she was giggling at the time.

And when Diana and Rosa Monckton were given the use of the Harrods jet to fly out for their holiday, Diana again reiterated the words as they surveyed the jet's plush interior. 'Oh, Rosa ... isn't it terrible?' she said, but again she was giggling like a schoolgirl.

A week after returning from the South of France, at the end of July, Diana agreed to spend the weekend with Dodi in Paris. During the two days they spent in the City of Love, they dined together at 3- or 4-star restaurants but Diana slept alone in the Imperial Suite at The Ritz Hotel while Dodi retired to his apartment.

The same scene was repeated a week later when Diana was invited to join Dodi on board the yacht *The Jonikal* for a Mediterranean cruise. Diana agreed only after being told she would have to leave KP for a short while as her rooms were being redecorated. Once again, the couple were assigned separate bedrooms.

Diana was happy with Dodi, of that there is no doubt; she told her stepmother Raine Spencer, in a satellite phone call, that he was a 'sweet, thoughtful man' and that she was 'blissfully happy'.

But for all the time they spent together, and the constant assertions from Mohammed Al Fayed since their deaths that they were due to get married, all the evidence points the other way. Diana actually went on the record and spoke to a journalist to stop the speculation. 'I have just got out of one marriage ... I am not jumping into another.'

And she is reported to have told a close friend, 'I need another husband like I need a bad rash.'

Again and again, Diana told friends she was having fun but that no marriage was planned. In fact, before her final, fatal holiday with Dodi, Diana phoned journalist Nigel Dempster and again bemoaned the constant gossip. Referring to the time she was spending away, she said, 'What does everyone expect ... that I spend the whole summer cooped up in Kensington Palace?'

At the end of August, Diana was due to go to Milan with her close friend American Lana Marks. Tragically, the trip was cancelled due to the death of Lana's father. Diana found herself at something of a loose end. Lana had returned to her family and there was nothing Diana could do. Rather than stay at KP, she accepted another invitation to join Dodi on board *The Jonikal*.

☞ *Go back into South Street and turn left into Park Street. After two blocks, turn right into Mount Street. The first building on the left is the Embassy of Brazil residency at number 54.*

Embassy of Brazil residency at number 54.

Embassy of Brazil

Of all the older, well-connected women to whom Diana turned to advice, none was more influential than Lucia Flecha de Lima, whom she met during an official visit to Brazil in 1991. With her own mother living in rural isolation on the Isle of Seil off the west coast of Scotland, Diana adopted women whose own children had grown up and who had time to nurture her. Flecha de Lima, then the wife

Strong links. Diana stands beneath the statue of Christ the Redeemer in Rio de Janiero, Brazil, in 1991.

of the Brazilian Ambassador to London, was just the kind of wise woman that Diana needed, and for a long time she was her mother figure, holding a special place in Diana's heart. Flecha de Lima, the eldest of nine children, had grown up in some style in a 44-room mansion with staff to match. Happily married since her teens, her stable influence saw Diana through some of her most difficult crises.

Their friendship followed the familiar, rather one-sided pattern of all Diana's friendships. Diana would call at all hours of the night or day, wrenching the kindly Flecha de Lima from dinner parties or dragging her out of bed for therapeutic chats. Entire weekends would be spent at the ambassadorial residence on Mount Street in Mayfair, where Diana would kick off her shoes and sample the sort of informal family life that had been denied her as a child and, lately, as an adult.

☞ *Step back into Park Street and continue northwards for a further four blocks until you reach Upper Brook Street. Turn left and Le Gavroche is the first doorway on the left.*

Le Gavroche

Leaving Le Gavroche after a lunch date.

Princess Diana always maintained that Mayfair restaurants come and go but that Le Gavroche never changed. To some extent, Diana's words are as relevant today, for the service at the Le Gavroche is, quite simply, the very best in London.

Head chef, the legendary Michael Roux Jnr, is ever present (a lesson for the so-called celebrity chefs of today) and the buttery-rich, classic French food continues to attain heights of gimmick-free perfection that other flashier joints can only dream of. The décor has changed very little since it was founded in the late 1960s.

One particular note of interest is that the original Gavroche was the urchin in one of Diana's favourite musicals, *Les Miserables*.

☞ *Turn around and walk back over Park Street, then continue along Upper Brook Street. After 100 metres, you will see the Embassy of The United States of America on your right. Walk into Grosvenor Square and walk diagonally across the centre into Carlos Place. The Connaught Hotel is 50 metres on your left.*

Connaught Hotel

Diana's favourite venue for lunch with Raine Spencer was the Connaught Hotel. Built in the latter part of the 19th century, the Connaught represents English hospitality at its best and has all the characteristics of Raine herself. The Connaught has an air of Edwardian elegance while maintaining the feel of an upper-class English home. The hotel, like Raine, belongs to a time and era that will never come again.

Relations with Raine Spencer were warming at the Connaught Hotel.

☞ *Retrace your steps and return to Grosvenor Square. Keep to the right side as you walk around it. When you reach Brook Street, turn right into it. Claridges is found on the right-hand side after approximately 100 metres.*

☞ *Continue for a further 100 metres until you reach New Bond Street. Turn right and walk down New Bond Street for about*

Diana looking stunning with her jewellery on a visit to Germany in 1987.

400 metres when you will reach a pedestrian area; continue across and, when you reach the other side, Asprey can be found on the right.

'With love from Diana'

William Asprey, descendant of Huguenot immigrants, set up his jewellers shop in 1781. The House of Asprey has held Royal Warrants from all reigning sovereigns since Queen Victoria in 1861 and today still holds a Royal Warrant to the Prince of Wales.

Diana came to the exclusive jewellers several weeks before she died and bought Dodi a gold cigar cutter, inscribed with the words 'With love, from Diana', which she gave to him along with some gold cufflinks, which once belonged to her father.

Asprey.

☞ *Return up New Bond Street, across the pedestrian area and, after a further 50 metres, turn left into Bruton Street. After 100 metres, you will arrive in Berkeley Square. Cross over the centre of the square to the opposite side, where you will see Annabel's basement nightclub.*

Annabel's nightclub in Berkeley Square.

Annabel's

Diana's favourite club, Annabel's, has the unique distinction of being London's first members-only nightclub. The venue was opened in 1963 by Mark Birley and named after his then wife Lady Annabel, who later married Sir James Goldsmith. Since then, Annabel's has been the most sought-after location for aristocrats, royalty and the super-rich. Apart from Diana, famous members and guests over the years have included Jackie Kennedy, Frank Sinatra, Elizabeth Taylor, Muhammad Ali and President Nixon. An honouree member is HM the Queen and it is still the only nightclub she has ever been to.

There is a strict dress code at the club – Prince Andrew was once turned away because he was not wearing a tie. In 1972, five years before Charles first met Diana, he met a young lady by the name of Camilla Shand at the club; the pair had originally met at a polo match a year before. They struck up a conversation and for some time became romantically involved. Unfortunately for Charles, Camilla Shand broke his heart just over a year later when she married army officer Andrew Parker Bowles.

In July 1986, Annabel's was supposed to have been the secret venue for Prince Andrew's stag night before his marriage to Sarah Ferguson. Diana and Fergie, along with Pamela Stephenson, dressed up as policewomen for Sarah's hen night and gatecrashed the club expecting to see Andrew's party. However, the Prince had moved the venue to a new secret address on the advice of his protection officers, but the girls stayed at the club until late anyway, drinking champagne cocktails.

☞ *Facing the entrance of Annabel's, turn left and walk down the side of the square. The square should be on your left-hand side. At the south-western corner of the square is Charles Street. Turn right and Mark's Club can be found 20 metres down on the left side of the street at number 46.*

Mark's Club

Mark's Club, literally just around the corner from Annabel's, is the third in the 'Holy Trinity' of private-members clubs Diana frequented (the other being Harry's Bar). Based in a serene Mayfair townhouse, Mark's Club prides itself on discretion and keeps its members insulated from the hectic pace of the city outside. Of course, this service doesn't come cheap, and it costs a £1,000 a year to be a member at Mark's, but they'll only take your money and allow you entry after you

Diana and Fergie leaving Mark's Club.

have been proposed and seconded by two existing members of the club.

Diana and Fergie would always use the quiet downstairs restaurant whenever the Duchess of York was visiting London (see page 7 plate section).

☞ *Return to Berkeley Square and turn right into Fitzmaurice Place. Walk for 20 metres until the road turns right. Turn left at this point into the passageway on your left called Lansdowne Row. At the end, cross over Berkeley Street into the road adjacent, Hay Hill. At the end of Hay Hill, turn right into Dover Street. Walk to the end of Dover Street, to the T-junction with Piccadilly. Across the road you will see The Ritz Hotel.*

Cross over Piccadilly and walk left, then turn right into St James's Street. Walk down St James's for 10 metres, then take

Diana was a regular visitor to the Ritz in 1983.

the first left into Jermyn Street. After walking along Jermyn Street
for 10 metres, Turnbull & Asser can be found on your right at
the junction of Bury Street.

Turnbull & Asser

Contrary to popular opinion, Diana and Dodi did not meet for the first time in the South of France in 1997, but many years before at exclusive shop Turnbull & Asser. The shop, founded in 1885 and still known as the best shirt maker in London, is owned by Mohammed Al Fayed's brother, and Dodi was a director.

Diana often shopped here while married to Charles, buying shirts for herself, as Charles had got tired of her taking his. Later, she also bought shirts here for James Hewitt. She became great friends with Ken Williams, the store manager known as 'the heart and soul of T & A'.

One day in 1985, she had come to the shop to buy pyjamas for her husband when she discovered a full board meeting was taking place upstairs. Coyly, Diana asked Ken, 'So what exactly goes on up there?'

Pointing up the stairway, Ken replied, 'Board meeting … boring.'

With a mischievous grin, Diana immediately raced up the stairs and gatecrashed the meeting, startling the various suits around the table as she declared, 'Ah-ha… so *this* is how you all waste your time.'

At the far end of the room sat Dodi, and that was the first time Diana ever set eyes on him.

☞ *To find your way to the nearest underground station – Green*
Park – return to Piccadilly and turn left past The Ritz Hotel.
Green Park is located directly after the hotel.

WALK 5

THIS WALK INCLUDES:

Houses of Parliament / The Cenotaph /
Downing Street / Horse Guards Parade / The Mall
/ St James's Palace / Clarence House / Spencer
House / Buckingham Palace / Guards Chapel /
Westminster Abbey.

Length – *2 miles or 3.2 km*
Time – *1½ hours*
Underground – *Westminster*
Bus routes – *3, 12, 53, 87, 88, 148, 159, 214,
453, 510 and C10.*

Getting to the starting point – Victoria Tower, Houses of Parliament,
Sovereign's Entrance, Houses of Parliament, Abingdon Street.

*Exit Westminster station on to Bridge Street. With the station behind you and
Big Ben in front of you, turn right and walk to the traffic lights. Turn left and
cross over the road. Continue along the west side of Parliament Square, keeping
The Houses of Parliament on your left. When you reach the end of the building,
you have reached the Victoria Tower and the Sovereign's Entrance.*

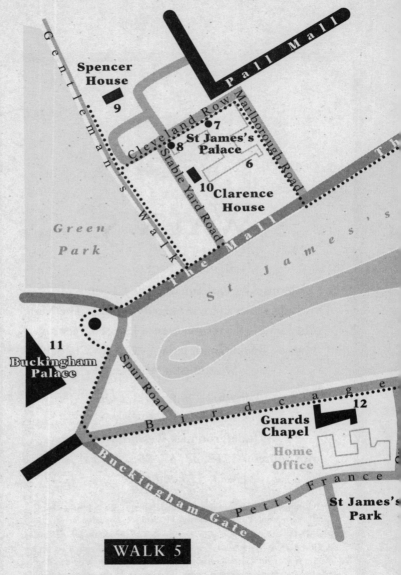

Spencer House

9

Pall Mall

Cleveland Row

Marlborough Road

7

8 **St James's Palace**

6

10 **Clarence House**

Stable Yard Road

Gentleman's Walk

Green Park

The Mall

St James's

J a m e s ' s

11

Buckingham Palace

Spur Road

B i r d c a g e

12 **Guards Chapel**

Home Office

Buckingham Gate

Petty France

St James's Park

WALK 5

START 1. Sovereign's Entrance, Palace of Westminster
2. Cenotaph
3. Home of the Prime Minister, 10 Downing Street
4. Archway into Horse Guards Parade
5. Horse Guards Parade / Trooping the Colour Parade Ground
6. St James's Palace
7. St James's Palace / Main Entrance, survives from Palace of Henry VIII

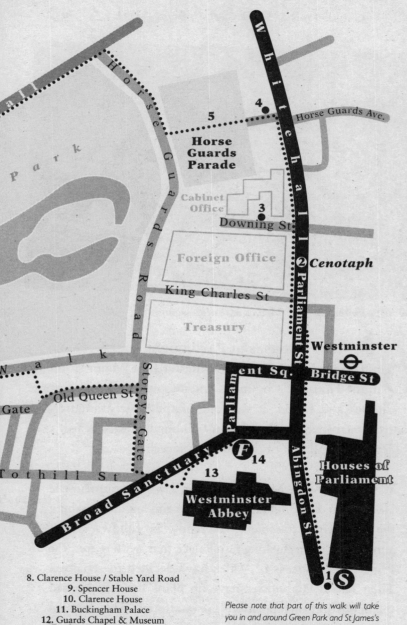

5

4

Whitehall

Horse Guards Ave.

Horse Guards Parade

Cabinet Office

3

Downing St.

Foreign Office

② *Cenotaph*

King Charles St

Treasury

Parliament St

Westminster ⊖

Walk

Old Queen St

Parliam'ent Sq. **Bridge St**

Gate

Storey's Gate

Tothill St

Broad Sanctuary

Ⓕ 14

13

Westminster Abbey

Abingdon St

Houses of Parliament

1 Ⓢ

Please note that part of this walk will take you in and around Green Park and St James's Park, which are open from 5am to midnight. The Mall is closed to traffic on Sundays.

Big Ben with the statue of Boudica in the foreground.

Houses of Parliament

On 9 December 1992, Prime Minister John Major stood up in the House of Commons and announced the separation of Charles and Diana. It was one of the most dramatic and controversial speeches the ancient building had ever heard.

Here is the full text of that historic speech:

With permission, Madam Speaker, I wish to inform the House that Buckingham Palace is at this moment issuing the following statement. It reads as follows: 'It is announced from Buckingham Palace that, with regret, the Prince and Princess of Wales have decided to separate. Their Royal Highnesses have no plans for divorce and their constitutional positions are unaffected. This decision has been reached amicably, and they will both continue to participate fully in the upbringing of their children.

'Their Royal Highnesses will continue to carry out full and separate programmes of public engagements, and will from time to time attend family occasions and national events together.

'The Queen and the Duke of Edinburgh, though saddened, understand and sympathise with the difficulties that have led to this decision. Her Majesty and his Royal Highness particularly hope that the intrusions into the privacy of the Prince and Princess may now cease. They believe that a degree of privacy and understanding is essential if their Royal Highnesses are to provide a happy and secure upbringing for their children, while continuing

Charles and Diana arrive at the Sovereign's Entrance for the state opening of Parliament, Westminster Palace, in 1991.

Charles and Diana on official duties.

to give a whole-hearted commitment to their public duties.'

At the end of the announcement, John Major then added his own words:

I am sure that I speak for the whole House – and millions beyond it – in offering our support to both the Prince and Princess of Wales. I am also sure that the House will sympathise with the wish that they should both be afforded a degree of privacy.

The House will wish to know that the decision to separate has no constitutional implications. The succession to the throne is unaffected by it: The children of the Prince and Princess retain their position in the line of succession and there is no reason why the Princess of Wales should not be crowned Queen in due course. The Prince of Wales' succession as head of the Church of England is also unaffected. Neither the Prince nor the Princess is supported by the civil list, and this position will remain unchanged.

I know that there will be great sadness at this news. But I know also that, as they continue with their royal duties and with bringing up their children, the Prince and Princess will have the full support, understanding and affection of the house and of the country.

☞ *With the Sovereign's Entrance behind you, walk north (right) towards Big Ben, keeping The Houses of Parliament on your right (those who have arrived by underground, retrace your steps to the pedestrian crossing). When you reach the corner of the street with Bridge Street and Big Ben to your right, continue across the pedestrian crossing and walk straight into Parliament Street. After 200 metres, on your left and in the centre of the road, you can find The Cenotaph.*

The Cenotaph

Each year, the Queen and senior members of the Royal Family attend the annual Service of Remembrance at the Cenotaph in Whitehall. The service, always held on the Sunday closest to 11 November, is to remember the dead of two world wars and the many other conflicts Britain has fought, and continues to fight. It is a time for solemn contemplation, when we are reminded that the freedom we take for granted was purchased with the blood, sweat and tears of so many others – men and

At the Cenotaph for the Remembrance ceremony of 1984. Left to right: Princess Diana, Princess Anne, Princess Alice and Elizabeth, the Queen Mother.

women who were prepared to pay the ultimate sacrifice: to lay down their lives for their country. Their memory is honoured so poignantly and tragically in the poem 'For the Fallen' that is read aloud by the Archbishop of Canterbury.

> They shall not grow old, as we that are left grow old
> Age shall not weary them, nor the years condemn
> At the going down of the sun and in the morning

We shall remember them. There follows two minutes' silence in memory of the fallen, and the Queen remembers: she remembers the dark days of May 1940, when France fell beneath the jackboot of the Nazis, and Great Britain stood alone. She remembers the immortal words of her own mother when the

The Queen pays her respects for the fallen in 1984.

suggestion was made to get the Royal Family to the safety of Canada: 'I will not leave the King, and the King will *never* leave the country.' She remembers those corners of a foreign field where brave men fell so others could be free – Normandy, Arnhem, Anzio, Burma, Dunkirk and all the other faraway places littered with the dead of the greatest generation the United Kingdom has ever produced. And finally, as the cannons boom across Hyde Park to signal the end of the silence, she raises her head in pride and remembers a time when one country, *her* country, stood defiantly in front of the greatest evil this world has ever seen and said, 'Come and have a go if you think you're hard enough.'

They did.

They weren't.

☞ *Further on your left across the road is 10 Downing Street (behind black gates).*

10 Downing Street

The Queen's favourite Prime Minister was Harold Wilson, the plump, white-haired, cherub-faced, pipe-smoking Labour leader who first entered Downing Street in 1964.

Her Majesty loved the refreshing openness of Mr Wilson and the fact that he holidayed in the Scilly Isles. After 13 years of Conservative rule, Mr Wilson and his pipe were a breath of fresh air.

Like most of the country, she had been aghast at the antics of the previous government and still smarted over the Suez crisis. Suez hurt Britain, reducing her almost overnight to a second-rate nation and, in the Queen's eyes, that was unforgivable.

Harold Wilson, Yorkshire born but the MP for Huyton, Merseyside, made a big deal of the fact that his constituency was so close to Liverpool; of course, in 1964, any public figure with the *remotest* connection to Liverpool made sure everyone knew it.

The Queen enjoyed her regular meetings with Prime Minister Wilson so much that she eventually invited him to spend time with her family at their Scottish retreat Balmoral. On one occasion, the pair famously washed and wiped up together, Her Majesty donning rubber gloves and rinsing the dishes and Wilson drying them.

The Queen's *least* favourite PM was Margaret Thatcher – in fact, like much of the country, she hated her. During the weekly meetings between the monarch and Thatcher, it was often asked, 'Exactly which one is royalty?'

On one occasion, Mrs Thatcher was far too busy to meet the Queen and sent a message saying she wouldn't be attending that day's meeting. The Queen was not at all happy and a member of her staff called Downing Street. They explained very politely that, although Her Majesty appreciated how busy the PM must be, as trying to rule the world was probably quite time consuming, it would be *very* advisable for her to be at Buckingham Palace that afternoon as arranged.

No one knows for sure what was said in reply but the meeting went ahead as scheduled with Mrs Thatcher in attendance.

☞ *Continue along Whitehall for about 200 metres until you reach the road on the right called Horse Guards Avenue. You should have arrived at a large building with two arches either side of a centre archway. Walk through the large centre archway on to Horse Guards Parade Ground.*

Horse Guards Parade

The Trooping of the Colour is the Queen's favourite ceremony, held on the parade ground at Horse Guards Parade to celebrate her official birthday on 2 June, and it is often referred to as the Queen's Birthday Parade. The highlight of the ceremony is the Trooping of the Colour, when the massed and magnificent ranks of the Guards Brigade march past Her Majesty as she takes the salute.

She attends every year. But terror came to the event on 13 June 1981, when a deranged young man fired a replica gun at the Queen as she rode past crowds on horseback. Marcus Serjeant, who was 17 at the time, pointed a pistol directly at the Queen as she turned down Horse Guards Parade for the start of the ceremony. He fired six blank cartridges before being overcome by

The Queen inspects the guards at the Trooping of the Colour at Horse Guards Parade in 1983.

The Queen and Princess Diana travel through the archway at Horse Guards Parade in 1991.

a guardsman and a police officer. The shots startled the Queen's horse but, with consummate skill, she was able to bring it back under control within a few seconds. Her Majesty looked shaken by the episode but soon recovered her composure.

Despite the pandemonium of the arrest, with uniformed police and guardsmen launching into the crowd to grab Serjeant, the procession continued as planned and afterwards the Queen returned to Buckingham Palace by the same route. Throughout the ordeal, her only concern had been for her 19-year-old horse, Burmese, which she had ridden in successive birthday parades since 1969.

Marcus Serjeant was jailed for five years under the 1842 Treason Act, a law not used since 1966. The former air cadet from Folkestone, Kent, was found guilty of wilfully discharging a blank cartridge pistol at the person of Her Majesty the Queen, with intent to alarm her.

Chillingly, the court was told that at one stage Serjeant had planned to kill the Queen but had failed to obtain a suitable lethal weapon.

He served more than three years in jail before being released in October 1984.

☞ *Make your way across the parade ground until you reach the road. Turn right on to Horse Guards Road. At the T-junction, turn left into The Mall.*

The Mall

The backbone and resilience of the British Royal Family was amply shown by Princess Anne during a remarkable incident in The Mall.

On the evening of 20 March 1974, the Princess Royal and her husband, Captain Mark Phillips, were returning to Buckingham Palace when their chauffeur-driven Rolls-Royce was forced to halt by another car, which blocked their route. A man leaped from the vehicle, a light-coloured Ford Escort, armed with a pistol, and began blasting the royal car. Terrified, Princess Anne and her husband dived for cover as a personal protection officer returned fire.

In a dramatic shoot-out, the PPO, Inspector James Beaton, was wounded. Also wounded was chauffer Alex Callender, one of the Queen's senior drivers, who had attempted to shield the Princess by jumping into the rear of the car.

As Princess Anne and her husband dived to the floor, more than two dozen rounds were exchanged in the ferocious street firefight. A police officer that had heard the shots and rushed to

Princess Anne was terrified by the attack.

The Queen with PPO, Inspector James Beaton, who was shot in the Mall attack and later received the George Cross for his bravery.

the scene was hit in the stomach, and a man passing in a taxi was also wounded.

The gunman, later identified as 26-year-old Ian Ball, forced open the rear door and, at gunpoint, ordered Princess Anne out of the vehicle. 'Come with me!' he shouted. 'I want £2 million for you.'

Aghast, Princess Anne retorted, 'Not bloody likely,' and then added, 'And I haven't got £2 million.'

Ball, who was perhaps not surprisingly diagnosed with serious mental-health problems, then fled the scene but was pursued by a police officer who brought him crashing to the ground with a heroic rugby tackle.

Princess Anne was shocked by the incident but, fortunately, unhurt.

In a government inquiry set up to investigate the incident, Princess Anne said the only thing that stopped her from hitting Ball was the thought that he would shoot her. 'It was so infuriating. I kept saying I didn't want to get out of the car. I nearly lost my temper with him but I knew that, if I did, I should hit him and he would shoot me.'

Ball was eventually prosecuted for the attempted murder of the Princess's detective, and various other offences.

It soon emerged the shooting was an attempt to kidnap the Princess to hold her to ransom, when a letter penned by Ball addressed to the Queen was found demanding £3 million for her release. The deranged assailant was sentenced to life imprisonment and placed in a mental hospital.

His attempt to kidnap Princess Anne remains the closest attempt anyone has made to abduct a senior member of the Royal Family.

☞ *Continue for 500 metres and cross over The Mall into Marlborough Road. As you walk up Marlborough Road, St James's Palace is on the left.*

St James's Palace

Henry VIII commissioned the building of St James's Palace on the site of a former leper hospital and it was dedicated to St James the Less. The Tudor building of red-brick walls surrounds four courtyards. On the north side is the main entrance, which is flanked by polygonal turrets. The tower survives from the original Henry VIII palace.

In 1698, after fire destroyed Whitehall Palace, William III and Mary II took up residency and it became the administrative centre of the monarchy, as it remains today. Several historic events have

The Throne Room at St James's Palace.

taken place here. After Mary I died there, her heart was buried in the Palace Chapel Royal. It is reputed that Elizabeth I spent a night within its walls while awaiting the Spanish Armada to sail up the English Channel. Oliver Cromwell turned it into barracks during the English Commonwealth period.

Today, St James's Palace is still very much a working establishment and is the base of the Royal Court. The Princess Royal and Princess Alexandra use the Palace as their London residence.

Before the funeral of Princess Diana in 1997, her brother, Earl Spencer, rehearsed the reading of his famous eulogy to Diana's coffin as it lay in the chapel. He revealed later that he heard a 'whisper of satisfaction' from her coffin. The Earl said, 'I read it to Diana's coffin, in the chapel at St James's Palace, and at the conclusion heard a whisper that sounded like satisfaction in that sad, sad, place.'

In his controversial speech, read during the funeral at Westminster Abbey, he promised that Princes William and Harry would be protected by 'blood family', which was seen as a swipe on the Royal Family. He also used his speech to mount a thinly veiled attack on them for stripping her of her royal status, describing her as a British girl who 'needed no royal title to continue to generate her brand of magic'.

☞ *Follow the building around to the left and this will bring you to Cleveland Row. Walk down to the end, keeping the Palace on your left and you will arrive at the security barrier for Clarence House. Clarence House (white building) can be seen further down the Stable Yard Road on the left-hand side beyond the barrier.*

Clarence House as seen from The Mall.

Elizabeth, the Queen Mother.

Clarence House

Clarence House is quite simply one of the most beautiful houses in London and, for more than 50 years, was the beloved London home of the Queen Mother. Situated on The Mall, within a stone's throw of Buckingham Palace, it is attached to St James's Palace and shares the Palace's gardens.

Today it is the official residence of Charles and Camilla. Princes William and Harry both have apartments in the sumptuous four-storey house, that is a palace in all but name, but their army duties mean they spend little time there.

Like all royal homes, Clarence House has a fascinating history. It was commissioned by William IV, who was the Duke of Clarence before he inherited the throne in 1830, and it was built between 1825 and 1827 by John Nash.

Like many people, the Duke of Clarence found St James's Palace too cramped, and, after he became King, William passed the house on to his sister, Princess Augusta Sophia, and, following her death in 1840, to Princess Victoria of Saxe-Coburg- Saalfeld, the mother of Queen Victoria.

Once established as a major royal residence, Clarence House became a much-sought-after venue. In 1866, it became the home of Queen Victoria's second son and fourth child, Alfred, Duke of Saxe-Coburg and Gotha and Duke of Edinburgh, until his death in 1900. Before they'd moved out his belongings, however, the house was taken over by his younger brother, Prince Arthur.

Arthur lived in the house until his death in 1942, during which time it suffered bomb damage. For the rest of the war, it was used by the Red Cross and the St John Ambulance Brigade as their headquarters, before being given to the young Princess Elizabeth and her husband, the Duke of Edinburgh, and Princess Anne was born there in 1950.

Following the death of George VI, Princess Elizabeth became Queen and moved up the road to Buckingham Palace. The vacated house was snapped up by the Queen Mother and Princess Margaret, who moved in together in 1953. Margaret eventually moved into Kensington Palace but the Queen Mum stayed at Clarence House until her death in 2002. Each year, on the Queen Mother's birthday, all members of the Royal Family would gather outside Clarence House for the traditional playing of 'Happy Birthday' by the Brigade of Guards.

The day before her engagement to Prince Charles was officially announced, Princess Diana moved into Clarence House. For three days, she was schooled in the art of royal protocol before moving into her own apartment in Buckingham Palace.

Charles and Diana unite for the Queen Mother's 89th birthday celebrations at the gates of Clarence House in 1989 (see also page 8 of the plate section).

To visit Spencer House

☞ *With the security barrier behind you, walk into Little St James's Street. Turn right after 30 metres, then turn left when you arrive at St James's Street. Walk up St James's Street for 10 metres and turn left into St James's Place. Spencer House is at number 27.*

After your visit, retrace your steps to Clarence House security barrier, then continue as below.

To continue the walk with a brief view of Spencer House
☞ *Continue onwards along Cleveland Row to Lugsmoor Lane. There is a passageway leading into Green Park. Walk down the passageway and turn right. Walk 20 metres and Spencer House is on your right.*

Spencer House

Spencer House was commissioned in 1756 for John, first Earl Spencer, an ancestor of Diana. Situated in the heart of St James's, Spencer House is a short distance from St James's Palace, Buckingham Palace and the Palace of Westminster, and has a splendid terrace and garden with magnificent views of Green Park. From its conception, Spencer House was recognised as one of the most ambitious aristocratic town houses ever built in London and is, today, the city's only great 18th-century private palace to survive intact.

> I do not apprehend there is a house in Europe of its size, better worth the view of the curious in architecture and the fitting up and furnishing great houses, than Lord Spencer's in St James's Place ... I know not in England a more beautiful piece of architecture ... in richness, elegance and taste, superior to any house I have seen.
>
> – Arthur Young, 1772

The Spencer family last lived in the house in 1926. They then let the building to a variety of tenants. As a result, the grand state

Spencer House.

rooms were used as offices from the late 1920s until 1985, when RIT Capital Partners acquired the lease.

☞ *Retrace your steps passing by the passageway on your left. Continue through Green Park towards The Mall. Turn left on The Mall and walk 20 metres. On your left is another view of Clarence House, now on the right-hand side of Stable Yard Road. About turn and continue up The Mall. Cross over to the Queen Victoria Memorial and Buckingham Palace.*

Buckingham Palace

Buckingham Palace is the biggest, grandest, most magnificent building in London and easily one of the most famous palaces in the world. Since 1837, it has served as the official London residence of Britain's sovereigns.

The Duke of Edinburgh once referred to Buckingham Palace as the 'flat above the office' for, as well as being the centrepiece of Britain's constitutional monarchy, it is very much a working building. Hundreds of royal staff are employed to support the day-to-day activities and duties of the Queen and the Duke of Edinburgh.

Princess Diana moved into Buckingham Palace after her engagement to Prince Charles was officially announced but she never found it a very welcoming place. Many a time Diana moaned to friends that she was left on her own and that the only solace she found was swimming in the Palace pool every morning.

After her separation from Prince Charles, Diana continued to use the pool but the privilege was taken away from her after her divorce, the Queen insisting that, as Diana had just made £17 million from the divorce, she could well afford her own pool.

The gates of Buckingham Palace.

☞ *Facing Buckingham Palace, walk to the furthest left-hand point of the Palace buildings along the fence. Then turn left into Birdcage Walk. After 200 metres, the Guards Chapel can be found behind the railings on the right-hand side of the street.*

Guards Chapel

The Guards Chapel, just south of St James's Park, has been the location of a military chapel since 1838. The first chapel was called the Royal Military Chapel and was built after Dr William Dakins, Chaplain to the Brigade of Guards, suggested that the troops have a separate place of worship of their own.

On Sunday, 18 June 1944 at 11am, during the morning service, the chapel was hit by a flying bomb that entered at the western end and exploded. It all but destroyed the building, only the apse being undamaged, and 121 people, soldiers and

A service at the Guards Chapel.

civilians, were killed with many others injured. The six silver candlesticks (a gift from George VI) and the cross, still used for normal services today, were in use at the time but were unmoved by the explosion, and the candles remained burning after the chapel had crashed in ruins.

The current building was constructed to replace the damaged chapel and was finished in 1963.

The Guards Chapel was the venue for a service to mark the tenth anniversary of Diana's death. Senior members of the Royal Family, including the Queen, Prince Charles and Prince Philip, joined Prince William and Harry at the emotional gathering.

In a poignant speech, Prince Harry told the congregation that Diana was 'the best mother in the world' and said, 'She made us and so many people happy.'

Harry, who was 12 when his mother was killed, said her death was 'indescribably shocking and sad', and changed his life and that of his brother forever. He added, 'When she was alive we completely took for granted her unrivalled love of life, laughter, fun and folly. We both think of her every day. We speak about her and laugh at all the memories.'

Prince William, who was 15 when Diana died, gave a reading from St Paul's letter to the Ephesians, which asked for inner strength. Diana's sister, Lady Sarah McCorquodale, also gave a reading. The service included Diana's favourite classical music by composers Rachmaninov and Mozart, and four hymns, concluding with Diana's favourite, 'I Vow to Thee My Country'. This beautiful and moving piece was also played at her wedding and her funeral.

Two notable absentees from the event were the Duchess of Cornwall and Mohammed Al Fayed.

Camilla decided not to attend despite being invited. She discussed the issue with William and Harry at length, and concluded that her presence would be a distraction.

Mr Al Fayed was not invited. Despite the fact that his son Dodi had died alongside Diana, his report to Lady Sarah that he had been given Diana's last words did not endear him to the Royal Family or the Spencers.

☞ *After approximately 150 metres, take the pathway through the gap in the fence. This will bring you into Old Queen Street. Turn left and walk to the end of the road. Turn right into Storey's Gate and follow it to the T-junction. At this point, you will be able to see Westminster Abbey across the road.*

Westminster Abbey

In 1064, England was ruled by Edward the Confessor, the son of Ethelred the Unready. Edward had grown up a confused and somewhat sad child of mixed cultures; his father was a Saxon and his mother, Emma, a Norman.

Ethelred died and his mother married the lunatic Dane, King Canute. Tactfully, Emma kept young Edward well away from his mad stepfather and had him farmed out to her own relations in Normandy. Therefore, although Edward was Saxon, he was brought up a Norman.

His best friend was an engaging young man called Duke William of Normandy (because of the peculiarities of this particular family's bloodline, he was also William's great-uncle). During one of those playful conversations all best friends have, Edward promised to make William his heir, a promise that was to have fearful repercussions for the country Edward was about to inherit.

In 1042, Edward's stepfather died during a heavy drinking session at a wedding feast. Few tears were shed for a man who had quickly taken up where his Viking predecessors had left off. King Canute continued to rape, plunder, murder and tax his own subjects even though there was no longer any need to do so. His name literally meant 'Deadly Cnut', which even a completely illiterate England could recognise as an obvious anagram.

Edward was 39 when he was brought back from Normandy and made King, a job for which he was ill prepared. As well as being terribly shy and not completely at ease with the English language, Edward was an albino and thus shied away from the day-to-day workings of the Royal Court.

He was regarded as more of a priest than a king and was never more comfortable than when talking to monks and abbots. Edward was a meek and mild man but he did have an uncanny ability to listen to others, thus his nickname, Edward the Confessor.

Leaving the job of running the country to others, Edward kept himself busy by building a glorious new abbey and a magnificent palace at a place called Westminster, near London. The name 'Westminster' means the 'monastery in the west' and, as it was well outside the city walls of London, that is how the locals called it.

Although Edward did live to see the completion of the abbey, he was far too ill to attend its opening ceremony on 28 December 1065, and rounded off a particularly miserable Christmas by dying a few days later on 5 January in the fateful year of 1066, when he had the distinction of becoming the first king to be buried at Westminster Abbey.

By all accounts, the Abbey was a busy place that day, for immediately after the funeral Edward's brother-in-law, Harold, sadly lacking in respect, had himself elected King and was crowned at one end of the Abbey while his predecessor's body was being entombed at the other.

Harold had no real claim to the throne except that he was Edward's brother-in-law, a tenuous link at best, as there were at least three other better-qualified claimants.

As Harold sat back in his throne and toasted his crown on his day of coronation, he contemplated his rivals. The first was Edgar the Atheling, descendant of Ethelred the Unready. He wasn't much of a problem; Atheling was only a boy and, therefore, a pushover.

Next up came Hardrada, King of Norway. Although Harold

Westminster Abbey and Victoria Tower, Palace of Westminster (rear right).

knew Hardrada would cause trouble, Norway was a long way away and the Norwegians, while still a ferocious and formidable foe, were no longer the force they used to be (Viking tactics were in many ways a forerunner of the *Blitzkrieg* campaigns launched by the Nazis – they were fine against an unprepared foe but next to useless against a well dug-in army).

Little boys and men with funny helmets Harold could handle but he knew the real threat came from just across the water, where Duke William of Normandy was preparing his claim for what, even in 1066, was already considered the greatest throne in the world.

And the rest, you can truly say, is history.

Princess Diana's funeral was held at Westminster Abbey on a day few will ever forget. The day of the funeral was bathed in bright sunshine. The coffin was draped in the Royal Standard and covered in lilies, a wreath of pink roses and the single posy of cream roses that broke the world's heart, as in front of it lay the hand-written card from Harry that read simply, 'Mummy'. As the coffin, borne on a gun carriage drawn by six black horses, reached St James's Palace, the royal men – Prince Charles, the Duke of Edinburgh and Princes William and Harry – stepped forward along with Earl Spencer to take their places behind the gun carriage.

To keep the boys from breaking down along the route, Philip talked to them quietly about each of the historic landmarks of London they passed. Landmarks their mother knew like the back of her hand.

The sombre procession, with the boys keeping their heads lowered, moved through Horse Guards Arch and down Whitehall towards Westminster Abbey.

Princess Diana's coffin is carried out from the Great West Door. Rex Features

The funeral cortege arrived at 11am by the Great West Door of the Abbey.

Inside the magnificent church, William and Harry stood side by side. Occasionally, one of them would wipe away a tear. Neither looked at the coffin. The most painful moment came right at the start of the service when Diana's favourite hymn, 'I vow to Thee My Country', was sung. Both being public schoolboys, Harry and William were as familiar with the words as their mother was and never failed to think of her when the hymn was sung at school. Now, with its quintessentially British tune that never fails to conjure up images of royalty, empire and a thousand years of history, the hymn seemed unbearably poignant, and the lyrics, 'the dearest and the best', sadly apt.

☞ *With the main entrance to Westminster Abbey behind you, turn right. Turn right again at the road, then follow the fence. The Abbey is on your right-hand side. Parliament Square is on your left. On your right, behind the fence, is St Margaret's Church.*

St Margaret's Church

On 8 October 1993, the church was the venue for the royal wedding of Viscount Linley, son of Princess Margaret and Antony Armstrong Jones, and the Honourable Serena Stanhope. Most members of the Royal Family, including Queen Elizabeth II and Princess Diana, attended the lavish wedding.

Viscount Linley and the Honourable Serena Stanhope are married in 1993.

☞ *When you have reached The Houses of Parliament in front of you, cross the road and turn left. Walk to the pedestrian crossing and cross over. At the other side of the road, turn right and walk up Bridge Street. Westminster underground station is on the left.*

Walk 5 Visitor information

The Houses of Parliament

Visitors who tour Parliament will see the key areas of the estate, such as the Commons and Lords debating chambers and the Queen's Robing Room. UK residents can tour throughout the year; overseas visitors may only tour during the summer opening. Accompanied by a trained guide, visitors travel through designated areas of the parliamentary estate. Tours take about 75 minutes.

• *www.parliament.uk*

St James's Palace

Not open to the public.

Clarence House

Clarence House is the official residence of The Prince of Wales and the Duchess of Cornwall and the home of Princes William and Harry. From 1953 to 2002, it was the home of Her Majesty Queen Elizabeth the Queen Mother.

Visitors are guided around the five ground-floor rooms, where the Prince of Wales and the Duchess of Cornwall undertake official engagements and receive guests from around the world.

The arrangement of the rooms and the grouping of their contents remain largely as they were in Queen Elizabeth's time, with much of Her Majesty's collection of works of art and furniture in their former positions. Clarence House also displays much of Queen Elizabeth's famous art collection, including outstanding 20th-century paintings including important works by John Piper,

Graham Sutherland, WS Sickert and Augustus John. Superb examples of Faberge, English porcelain and silver, particularly pieces relating to the Bowes-Lyon family, are also on display.

- *Telephone: 020 7766 7303*
- *Email: bookinginfo@royalcollection.org.uk*
- *By underground: Green Park or St James's Park*
- *By bus: Numbers 8, 9, 14, 19, 22 and 38 stop at Green Park*

Spencer House

Spencer House, London's most magnificent private palace, is open to the public for viewing every Sunday (except during January and August) from 10.30am–5.45pm.* Access is by guided tour, which lasts approximately one hour. Tours begin at regular intervals and the last admission is at 4.45pm. The maximum number of visitors on each tour is 20. It is recommended that visitors telephone before arriving as times are subject to change.

- *Telephone: 020 7499 8620*

Buckingham Palace

Buckingham Palace serves as both the office and London residence of Her Majesty the Queen, as well as the administrative headquarters of the Royal Household. It is one of the few working royal palaces remaining in the world today.

Today, the state rooms are used extensively by the Queen and members of the Royal Family to receive and entertain their guests on State, ceremonial and official occasions. During August and September, when the Queen makes her annual visit to Scotland, the Palace's 19 state rooms are open to visitors.

The state rooms form the heart of the working palace and are lavishly furnished with some of the greatest treasures from the Royal Collection: paintings by Rembrandt, Rubens, Poussin and Canaletto; sculpture by Canova; exquisite examples of Sèvres porcelain; and some of the finest English and French furniture.

The Palace's garden, described as a 'walled oasis in the middle of London', is home to 30 different species of bird and more than 350 different wild flowers, some extremely rare. Visitors end their tour with a walk along the south side of the garden, with splendid views of the west front of the Palace and the famous lake.

- Telephone: +44 (0)20 7766 7300
- Email: bookinginfo@royalcollection.org.uk
- Opening hours: 9.45am–6pm (last admission 3.45pm)
- By underground: Victoria, Green Park and Hyde Park Corner
- By bus: Numbers 11, 211, 239, C1 and C10 stop on Buckingham Palace Road

The Royal Mews at Buckingham Palace

One of the finest working stables in existence, the Royal Mews at Buckingham Palace provides a unique insight into the department of the Royal Household that provides transport by road for the Queen and other members of the Royal Family.

The Royal Mews houses the sate vehicles, both horse-drawn carriages and motorcars, used for coronations, sate visits, royal weddings, the State Opening of Parliament and official engagements. Visitors can see the Gold State Coach, which was last used during the Queen's Golden Jubilee in 2002 to carry Her Majesty and Prince Philip to the Service of Thanksgiving at St Paul's Cathedral.

For most of the year, the stables are home to the working horses that play an important role in the Queen's official and ceremonial duties. They are mainly Cleveland Bays, the only British breed of carriage horse, and the Windsor greys, which by tradition always draw the carriage in which the Queen is travelling. As they may be on duty, undergoing training or having a well-deserved rest away from London, the horses are not always on view.

- Telephone: 020 7766 7302
- Email: bookinginfo@royalcollection.org.uk

Guards Chapel

Monday–Thursday 10am–4pm, Friday 10am–2pm, Sunday 11am for services. Visitors are requested to telephone beforehand to check opening times as there are sometimes private services.

- Telephone: +44 (0)20 7414 3228

Westminster Abbey

Westminster Abbey is steeped in more than 1,000 years of history. Benedictine monks first came to this site in the middle of the tenth century, establishing a tradition of daily worship, which continues to this day. The Abbey has been the coronation church since 1066 and is the final resting place of 17 monarchs.

The present church, begun by Henry III in 1245, is one of the most important Gothic buildings in the country, with the medieval shrine of an Anglo-Saxon saint still at its heart.

A treasure house of paintings, stained glass, pavements, textiles and other artefacts, Westminster Abbey is also the place where some of the most significant people in the nation's history are buried or commemorated. Taken as a whole, the tombs and memorials comprise the most significant single collection of monumental sculpture anywhere in the United Kingdom.

The Library and Muniment Room houses the important (and growing) collections of archives, printed books and manuscripts belonging to the Dean and Chapter of Westminster, providing a centre for their study and for research into all aspects of the Abbey's long and varied history.

- *Telephone: +44 (0)20 7222 5152*
- *Email: info@westminster-abbey.org*
- *www.westminster-abbey.org/home*

OTHER
PLACES AND
PEOPLE OF
INTEREST

St Paul's Cathedral © Alex Harvey.

St Paul's Cathedral

On 29 July 1981, St Paul's Cathedral was the venue for the wedding of Prince Charles and Princess Diana. Over half a million people, hoping for a glimpse of the couple, lined the procession route from Buckingham Palace to St Paul's. The ceremony was watched by 3,500 invited guests and over 750 million television viewers worldwide. This was the most viewed TV programme of all time.

Charles and Diana leave St Paul's at their wedding 1981. Rex Features

A cathedral dedicated to St Paul has stood on the site since 604AD and, throughout, the cathedral has remained a busy, working church where millions come to reflect and find peace. St Paul's is not only an iconic part of the London skyline but also a symbol of the hope, resilience and strength of the city and nation it serves. Above all, St Paul's Cathedral is a lasting monument to the glory of God.

The nearest underground station is St Paul's on the Central line (a two-minute walk). Mansion House and Cannon Street stations on the District and Circle lines are also within walking distance. Central-line trains run every four minutes on weekdays and every six minutes at weekends.

- Bus routes: 4, 8, 11, 15, 17, 23, 25, 26, 76, 100, 172 and 242
- For further information visit www.stpauls.co.uk

Prince Charles competes in the father's race.

Prince William wins the obstacle race.

Richmond Athletic Ground

When Prince William and Prince Harry attended Wetherby School, Notting Hill, in the mid- to late 1980s, the annual parents' sports days were held at Richmond Athletic Ground. Princess Diana, with her keen spirit of adventure, always gleefully took part, competing in the Mothers' Sprint Race. Inevitably, with her daily workouts at the Chelsea Harbour Club, Diana always arrived first at the finishing tape ... much to her great pleasure.

Supported by her husband, Prince Charles, the royal couple made every effort to make their children's school sports day an enjoyable day out despite the troubles in their marriage (see page 7 plate section).

- *The nearest tube station is Richmond on the District line*
- *For further information visit www.the-raa.co.uk*

Susie Orbach

Princess Diana consulted psychotherapist Susie Orbach after suffering from the eating disorder bulimia. After driving alone in her Audi convertible to Orbach's North London office, Diana would spend two hours undergoing treatment for the condition.

In her book *Fat is a Feminist Issue*, the therapist, an expert in her field, blames men for causing women's emotional problems. The Princess first contacted Orbach after Prince Charles went public about his affair with Camilla Parker Bowles.

- *The nearest tube stations are Belsize Park and Swiss Cottage*
- *Bus routes are 268, 31, C11, N28 and N31.*

The world's no. 1 royal fan

A visit to the house of Margaret Tyler is a must for any royal devotee. Tucked away in a small suburban street in Wembley is Heritage House. From the outside it looks the same as many of the other houses in the street but, after entering through the front door, you will discover a vast labyrinth of

In a quiet north London street, Diana heads for her car after visiting psychotherapist Susie Orbach.

Margaret Tyler and her amazing Royal collection.

royal memorabilia other royal enthusiasts could only dream of collecting.

The magnificent 'Royal Collection' includes a Princess Diana shrine and a life-size throne, as well as a life-size cutout royal carriage. Margaret has collected over 20,000 items from the world over, the majority of which are extremely rare and extraordinary. The collection is now estimated to be worth over £150,000 at auction.

For a limited period, Margaret has decided to open the doors of Heritage House and share with royal fans an exclusive viewing of this remarkable collection. A rare opportunity not to be missed by any Diana and British Royal Family admirer.

All viewings are by appointment only. Margaret Tyler will give visitors a guided tour of the Royal Collection in return for a small financial contribution.

Bed and continental breakfast are available at £35 per night and the package includes a one-hour tour of Margaret's collection.

- *To make an appointment for a tour or bed & breakfast, telephone +44 (0)20 8904 2452 from 9am to 5pm.*

The Great Ormond Street Hospital

The hospital was founded in 1852 and is a hospital for the care of sick children – the first of its kind to provide in-patient beds specifically for children. Part of its funding nowadays comes from the ownership of copyright to Peter Pan, which was given to the hospital by the Scottish author and dramatist JM Barrie.

Princess Diana became Patron of the Great Ormond Street Hospital in 1989 after previously being involved in the

Mother love. Prince William is driven from Great Ormond Street hospital after treatment to a head injury in 1991.

Diana meets the children in the wards during an official visit in 1994

launching of The Wishing Well Appeal, raising money for a new hospital building.

Prince Charles was once treated at the hospital during his education at Cheam School in Berkshire, when he was suffering from appendicitis, and during an official royal visit in 2006, accompanied by the Duchess of Cornwall, he said, 'I have really remarkably happy memories of being here myself, long ago,' adding that he was 'happily operated on and looked after by the nurses'.

On 3 June 1991, Prince William was also treated at Great Ormond Street while at Ludgrove School, after a friend accidentally hit him over the head with a golf club. He was admitted for an operation, suffering from a depressed fracture on his skull, after being transferred by ambulance from the Royal Berkshire Hospital. Princess Diana was distraught and comforted

William, holding his hand during the drive home after the extensive treatment.

During an interview in March 2009, William disclosed details of his visit to the hospital to Alice, a ten-year-old cancer patient from the Royal Marsden Hospital. 'That was for my Harry Potter scar, as I call it, just here. I call it that because it glows sometimes and some people notice it – other times they don't notice it at all.'

His brother, Prince Harry, was also treated at the hospital for a hernia operation in 1988, aged three.

After numerous visits, some public, some private, Princess Diana made her final visit to open the Renal Unit in 1997 for the hospital's 145th birthday.

- *Great Ormond Street Hospital, Great Ormond Street, London WC1N 3JH*
- *The two nearest stations to GOSH are Russell Square (Piccadilly line) and Holborn (Piccadilly and Central lines).*
- *Neither station has disabled access, as they have steps leading to the platforms.*
- *Various buses come within 15 minutes' walk of the hospital, including route numbers 7, 8, 17, 19, 25, 38, 45, 46, 55, 59, 68, 91, 168, 188, 242, 243 and 521*
- *To make a donation to Great Ormond Street Hospital for Children visit www.gosh.org/donate/*

LA Fitness, Isleworth

In November 1993, Princess Diana was photographed by a 'peeping-tom' camera while exercising at her gym, the LA Fitness Club in Isleworth. The photographs were published by the *Sunday Mirror* and the *Daily Mirror*, causing widespread public outrage. The pictures, taken by the gym owner Bryce Taylor, showed the Princess clad in cycling shorts and leotard with her legs in the air on a workout machine called 'The Throne'. The hidden pinhole camera was placed in the ceiling just above the workout machine and set to take photographs on a timer.

Diana played sport or went to the gym on a daily basis.

Lawyers acting for the Princess started legal action against Mirror Group Newspapers, the gym and the gym's owner Bryce Taylor. The decision by Diana's legal action marked a significant new approach by a member of the British Royal Family in using the law to defend itself.

Mirror Group Newspapers were forced to apologise after a public backlash and a drop in sales. The LA Fitness Club apologised publicly in June 1994 and the action was dropped against them.

In February 1995, Bryce Taylor also apologised and returned the £300,000 he had earned from the photographs worldwide. A settlement was agreed on and it was believed that Mirror Group Newspapers paid Diana's legal costs of approximately £1 million and also £200,000 to Diana's choice of charities.

- *Swan Street, Old Isleworth, Middlesex TW7 6RJ*
- *The nearest underground station is Richmond*
- *Telephone: 020 8568 8844*
- *Email: isleworth@lafitness.co.uk*

Chelsea Harbour Club

It was Oliver Hoare who introduced Diana to the Harbour Club, on the banks of the Thames, early in 1993. Conscious of her isolation in KP, Diana resolved to combine her fitness obsession with a search for new friends. For her, as for many others, the gym operated in many ways like a social club. The only snag was that it was a club in which many of the members were married, including Hoare and Will Carling.

The Harbour Club is one of the most exclusive health clubs in the country and the one in which Diana was most likely to meet the right set of people: international types, business types, people from the right background and, most importantly, good-looking, body-conscious folks.

Diana joined not only to have some sort of normal contact with people, but also to be seen and to get some adoration for herself and her body. Her hair was always perfect when she went to the gym; while most women had theirs up in a ponytail or under a baseball cap prior to a good workout, Diana's hair was always on show and always looked great.

Diana always wore make-up as well. Her look always said 'look at me, see how gorgeous I am and how perfectly toned I am', as opposed to the girls in the baggy T-shirts.

The Harbour Club was all about being seen; showing what you had to those who already had it; it was the ultimate in metropolitan gyms. Mercedes, BMWs and Range Rovers filled the 80-space car park.

But being seen at the Harbour Club didn't come cheap. Diana (through Prince Charles's office) made a down payment of £2,600 for membership and a further £100 a month to use the facilities. Though expensive, the club was perfect for Diana and reflected the well-heeled, affluent existence she lived.

In the reception area, a polished wooden floor leads to the computerised entry system. Through the glass wall to the left can be seen the indoor tennis courts and the magnificent swimming pool, lined with tiles in the club's trademark dark blue. On the right is the crèche and the restaurant–bar, which serves appetising but transistorised meals, calculated to appeal to calorie-conscious members like Diana. French windows open out on to a terrace, where around 30 people can eat outside under shades in the summer.

After Diana's workout, she would head not for the showers and hair dryers of the changing room, but for the social area, where members meet over coffee. Then she would leave, looking

Diana was a keen tennis player at Chelsea Harbour Club.

Prince Harry and Prince William are driven from the Chelsea Harbour Club by their mother with the top down.

perfect for the ever-vigilant paparazzi who were lined up against the wall outside.

Although Diana did not socialise too much with the other members of the club, she did become great friends with the English rugby captain Will Carling, one of Britain's best-known and most popular sportsmen. In fact, she had met him before when she had been the guest of honour at rugby internationals. Within a few weeks of meeting, Diana and Carling had become so close that they gave each other nicknames. She called him 'Captain', while he called her 'the Boss'. In March 1995, Carling arranged for Princes William and Harry to attend an England get-together before the Rugby Union World Cup finals in South Africa. The boys were thrilled and so was Diana (see page 8 plate section).

Will Carling and Diana make a quick exit from the Chelsea Harbour Club.

Unfortunately for everyone concerned, Will Carling's bride of three months, Julia Carling, wasn't so happy with the relationship. When the story of Carling and Diana's friendship broke in the newspapers, an angry Julia accused Diana of trying to wreck her marriage. In vain, Will Carling insisted that his relationship with

Diana was wholly innocent, going on record to say, 'It was a perfectly harmless friendship with the Princess of Wales.'

Julia Carling continued to hark on about Diana and gave an extraordinary interview to the media, where she claimed Diana had picked the wrong couple to come between this time.

Alas, it was all to no avail. Carling continued to see Diana on and off throughout the autumn of 1995 and, inevitably, Will Carling and his wife broke up. After yet another meeting at the Harbour Club between the Captain and the Boss, it was announced that, with regret, Will and Julia Carling had 'agreed to spend some time apart'.

With supreme irony, the friendship between Carling and Diana came to an abrupt end at the same time. Diana, bored and angered with all the negative press she was suddenly receiving, realised she was no longer interested in the England rugby hero.

The nearest station is Fulham Broadway, then take a taxi (approx. one mile) to the Harbour Club.

- *Harbour Club, Watermeadow Lane, London SW6 2RR*
- *Telephone: 0845 125 7004*
- *www.harbourclubchelsea.com*

Heathrow Airport

Towards the end of her life, Susie Kassem was one of Diana's closest friends. Kassem, a retired magistrate and hospital visitor, had met the Princess at the Brompton Hospital in the summer of 1996.

They were together on the fateful day that Hasnat Khan stepped into the lift they were sharing and Diana saw the man who was to be her last great love for the first time.

Great friends Diana and Susie Kassem in Sydney Street.

'Her knees literally went weak,' said Susie. 'She told me he was "drop-dead gorgeous".'

It was Susie that drove Diana to Heathrow Airport during the bank holiday weekend of 1996, when Diana attempted to fly to Spain to discuss buying her love letters back from James Hewitt. She accompanied Diana to the Iberia check-in for the flight to Alicante. After getting her boarding pass, Diana and Susie headed for the Bureau de Change to buy pesos. In the departure lounge, they were spotted by the photographers who keep a round-the-clock vigil for travelling celebrities, and the pair took refuge in the ladies lavatories for 15 minutes, until Diana boarded the plane and set off for Spain.

On the last day of her life, Diana phoned Susie three times. During the final call, made late in the afternoon, Diana told her she could not wait to get home and see her boys. They then arranged to meet at the small café in Chelsea Farmer's Market, next to Brompton Hospital, on the Tuesday morning.

Tragically, it was a date Diana never kept.

Leicester Square

As well as the Odeon cinemas in Kensington High Street and Fulham Road, Diana also watched movies in Leicester Square, both publicly and also very privately. In the tree-filled oasis of Leicester Square, the Princess outshone the top Hollywood stars at the big film premieres, where many of the new movies are first aired to royalty and the glitterati in either the Empire or the Odeon. Celebrity A-listers from Hollywood, including Clint Eastwood, Liza Minnelli and Barbra Streisand, often rubbed shoulders with Diana and other royalty as their latest releases were premiered.

At the 1992 UK premiere of Hook *Diana meets stars Robin Williams and Dustin Hoffman at the Odeon in Leicester Square.*

Diana in the spotlight at the premiere of Amadeus *at the Odeon Leicester Square.*

On many occasions, Diana would privately slip out from Kensington Palace with sons William and Harry to see an afternoon movie in the square. Arriving with police protection officers, the threesome went almost unnoticed as they arrived to see *Jurassic Park* among the throng of tourists visiting London's entertainment hub.

• *The nearest underground station is Leicester Square.*

Diana meets movie legend Clint Eastwood at the premiere of The Fugitive *in 1993.*

Princess Diana's spiritualist

Betty Palko – spiritual consultant to Princess Diana.

The Irish clairvoyant Betty Palko was Diana's spiritual consultant from 1987, and the Princess visited her suburban South London home on a regular basis.

After the death of Diana's father, Earl Spencer, he allegedly manifested himself in his daughter's presence. The Princess could not see or hear him but she was convinced that he was present when, through Mrs Palko, he referred to family matters that the medium presumably could not have known. He also apparently appeared to Mrs Palko while she was at prayer, and informed her that his daughter would change the face of the monarchy. 'I see her as Queen,' he is said to have told her.

'He gave me a message of love and understanding for her,' the clairvoyant explained. 'And [he] apologised for leaving at a time when she needed him.'

• *To book an appointment for a reading, visit www.bettypalko.com*

Diana was a regular visitor to Betty Palko.